Celebration Cakes

Celebration Cakes

Easy-to-decorate cakes for every occasion

KAREN GOBLE

NEW HOLLAND

First published in 2005 by New Holland Publishers (UK) Ltd
London · Cape Town · Sydney · Auckland

Garfield House, 86–88 Edgware Road, London, W2 2EA, United Kingdom
www.newhollandpublishers.com

80 McKenzie Street, Cape Town 8001, South Africa

14 Aquatic Drive, Frenchs Forest, NSW 2086, Australia

218 Lake Road, Northcote, Auckland, New Zealand

ISBN 1 84330 977 7

Senior Editor: Clare Hubbard
Editorial Direction: Rosemary Wilkinson
Design: Sara Kidd
Photographer: Shona Wood
Production: Ben Byram-Wigfield

1 3 5 7 9 10 8 6 4 2

Reproduction by Colourscan Overseas Co, Pte Ltd, Singapore
Printed and bound in Malaysia, by Times Offset (M) Sdn, Bhd

Note
The author and publishers have made every effort to ensure that all instructions
given in this book are safe and accurate, but they cannot accept liability for any
resulting injury or loss or damage to either property or person, whether direct or
consequential and howsoever arising.

Because of the slight risk of salmonella, raw eggs should not be served to the very young,
the ill or elderly, or to pregnant women.

In the recipes use either metric or imperial measurements, but never a combination of the two,
as exact conversions are not always possible.

ACKNOWLEDGEMENTS
I would like to thank:
Lesley Tanner, who has helped in typing up my text and tried and tested all of the recipes.

Culpitt Limited and Renshaw Scott Ltd for their help in supplying materials, tools and equipment.
Major Johnson for supplying unusual shaped dummies and boards.

New Holland Publishers, for asking me to do this book.

Contents

Introduction

When you think of all the different celebrations that family and friends have – birthdays, christenings, weddings, anniversaries – they all have one thing in common: a cake. It is always the focal point of the party. This book contains 40 wonderful cakes for every occasion you can think of, so you can create your own centrepiece to be proud of.

I have included cakes made using buttercream, sugarpaste (rolled fondant), royal icing and chocolate, in a wide variety of styles and shapes, so there is something for everyone here. All of the cakes are suitable for beginners and more experienced cake-makers alike. If you are new to cake decorating don't be put off by the elaborate appearance of some of the finished cakes. That's the whole point of this book – to show you the stunning results that can be achieved using basic skills.

It has been a pleasure for me to design and make the cakes for this book. I hope that you are inspired and experience delight and pleasure when producing a cake for that special occasion.

Equipment

Here is a list of the tools and equipment that I used when making the cakes in this book. Many of the items are part of the basic 'kit' that any cake decorator needs, others you will only use now and again. Get to know your gadgets, as many of them can be used in a variety of ways.

Cake tins (pans) It is useful to have an assortment of shapes and sizes to hand.

Clingfilm (plastic wrap) Use to cover pastes and icings as it stops them from drying out and keeps them fresh.

Cocktail sticks Use to add colour to icing.

Crimpers Use to create a pattern in sugarpaste on cakes and boards. Various types available.

Cutters A vast range of shapes is available in both plastic and metal – stars, flowers, hearts etc.

Dust colours Mainly used to add colour to sugar flowers.

Electric mixer Essential piece of time-saving equipment.

Acetate Useful when making royal icing runouts. Can also be used for stencils.

Bowls You will need a variety of bowls for mixing cake mixture, icings etc.

Cake boards Come in a wide variety of shapes and sizes, generally silver or gold in colour.

Cake leveller Used to level the top of the cake and also to split the cake horizontally.

Embossers Create a pattern in sugarpaste – can be used to great effect on cakes and boards.

Greaseproof (waxed) paper Essential for the cake maker and decorator. Used for wrapping cakes, lining tins and making piping bags and templates.

Icing comb Used for combing royal icing or buttercream onto a cake.

Moulds Come in all shapes and sizes, useful for modelling.

Non-stick mat Useful when assembling small elements – flowers/models etc. as paste slides off mat easily.

Paintbrushes Used for painting and adding delicate details. Also used for applying dust colours.

Palette knife An absolute must-have. Useful for spreading, mixing and lifting.

Paste colours These are more concentrated than liquid colours and do not make your icings/pastes sticky.

Piping (pastry) bags Greaseproof paper, reusable and disposable piping bags are available.

Piping tubes (nozzles) These come in all shapes and sizes and are used for piping.

Rolling pins Come in all sizes. Use a large one for rolling out big pieces of sugarpaste for covering cakes and boards and a small one for flowers, modelling etc. I would recommend using non-stick.

Scissors Make sure they are sharp – used for making piping bags, cutting linings for tins etc.

Sharp knife Another must-have item. Useful for trimming sugarpaste from around boards.

Side scraper Used for smoothing royal icing around the sides of the cake.

Smoother Eliminates lumps and bumps from sugarpaste and marzipan to give the cake a professional finish.

Spirit level To start with, use to check that your oven is level. Mainly used for checking that cakes are level.

Straight edge I use this for levelling the tops of my royal-iced cakes.

Sugarcraft gun Extrudes lengths of sugarpaste and marzipan. A variety of discs available to create different designs.

Sugarcraft tools There are so many tools on the market today – they are very useful for modelling.

Tape I mainly use two sorts of tape: paper floristry tape for binding flowers and sprays and double-sided tape to attach ribbon around cake boards.

Tape measure/ruler You will use this all the time.

Textured rollers There are many patterns available and they give a fantastic effect when used on sugarpaste.

Turntable There are many different turntables on the market but I find one that can tilt is most useful as it makes it easier when working on the side of the cake.

Tweezers Both straight and angled tweezers are available.

Veiners Enable you to get a realistic effect on leaves and petals.

Veining board When paste is rolled over board a vein is created into which wire can be inserted.

Wires The thickness of wire is referred to as the gauge. The higher the gauge the finer the wire.

4 Add glycerine to the mixture if you are using the icing for coating or if a softer icing is required. The icing should be light and fluffy.

5 Place the icing into a sealable container and directly cover the surface of the icing with clingfilm before placing on the lid. Keep for a maximum of two days.

Alternative Royal Icing Recipe

10g (½oz) dried egg white

60ml (4 Tbsp) water

450g (1lb/3 cups) icing (confectioner's) sugar

5ml (1 tsp) glycerine

1 Mix the dried egg white and water together thoroughly in a small container. Leave to stand for about 5 minutes.

2 Sieve the icing sugar thoroughly.

3 Sieve the dried-egg white mixture into a large mixing bowl and add one third of the icing sugar. Mix until the icing sugar is absorbed.

4 Continue adding small amounts of sugar until it has all been used, mixing well after each addition.

5 Add the glycerine to the mixture, if you are using the icing for coating, and mix well.

6 Place the icing into a sealable container and directly cover the surface of the icing with clingfilm before placing on the lid.

Making a Piping (Pastry) Bag

1 Cut some greaseproof paper into a triangle.

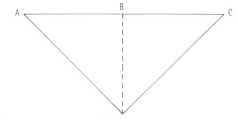

2 Pick up corner C and fold over, so that B forms a sharp cone in the centre.

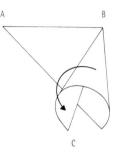

3 Wrap corner A around the cone. Make sure that A and C are at the back and that the point of the cone is sharp.

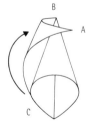

4 Fold points A and C inside the top edge of the bag to hold it securely. Snip off the end B and insert a piping tube.

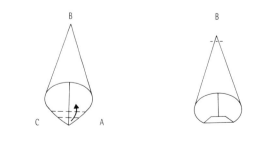

Colouring Royal Icing

You can use various products to colour your icing but do make sure the correct consistency is maintained.

1 Mix the icing thoroughly.

2 Add the food colouring to the royal icing a little at a time using a cocktail stick (pic a).

3 Stir or mix the colouring into the icing until blended (pic b).

4 Leave the icing to stand to allow the colour to mature.

5 Place icing into a sealable container. Directly cover the surface of the icing with clingfilm before placing on the lid.

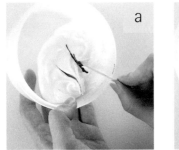 

Marzipan (Almond Paste)

Marzipan (almond paste) can be used for coating and modelling. It forms a smooth coating on a cake and makes a perfect base for sugarpaste or royal icing, forming a barrier that prevents moisture seeping from the cake into the coating. For modelling the paste is pliable and easy to handle and can be coloured in the same way as sugarpaste by kneading in food colourings (see page 15). Store in a polythene bag until ready for use. It is advisable to use the marzipan within one week.

225g (8oz/1½ cups) icing (confectioner's) sugar
225g (8oz/1½ cups) ground almonds
1 large egg white (see note page 4)
1 tsp lemon juice
Few drops almond essence (extract)

1 Place the icing sugar and ground almonds into a bowl, add the egg white, lemon juice and almond essence and stir together.

2 Knead the mixture until smooth on a surface dusted with icing sugar.

Flower Paste

Flower paste dries hard and is normally used for making flowers and leaves. For this recipe you will need an electric mixer.

450g (1lb/3¼ cups) icing (confectioner's) sugar
15ml (3 tsp) gum tragacanth
10ml (2 tsp) powdered gelatine
25ml (5 tsp) cold water
10ml (2 tsp) white vegetable fat (shortening)
10ml (2 tsp) liquid glucose
1 large egg white (see note page 4)

1 Sift the icing sugar and gum tragacanth.

2 Place the icing sugar and gum tragacanth together into a mixing bowl and warm in a very low oven (150°C/300°F/Gas mark 2) for around 5 minutes.

3 Dissolve the gelatine in the cold water and leave to stand until no grains are left.

4 Add the white vegetable fat and liquid glucose to the gelatine.

5 Dissolve over hot (not boiling) water or in a microwave on defrost or the lowest setting (do not allow to boil).

6 Put the icing sugar into a warmed bowl and add the gelatine mixture and egg white.

7 Mix together until white and 'stringy'.

8 Knead the mixture together by hand, then knead on a work surface lightly dusted with icing sugar.

9 Wrap in two layers of clingfilm and place in a polythene bag. Leave to stand for 24 hours before using.

Flower Paste Glue

This is a clear glue and is mainly used to secure wire in flowers and leaves.

> 1.25ml (¼ tsp) Tylo powder (a thickener)
> Water

1 Put the Tylo powder into a small, sealable pot. Cover the powder with cold water and leave to dissolve.
2 Stir until the mixture is thick and clear. Add more water or powder to achieve the correct consistency.
3 Place the top on the pot. The mixture is ready for use as required.

Modelling Paste

This is a paste for making models and decorations. Gum tragacanth acts as a strengthening agent, so it sets much harder than sugarpaste and holds its shape. If rolling out the paste work on a surface dusted with a little icing sugar. When modelling small pieces use a smear of white vegetable fat on your fingers to prevent sticking.

> 280g (10oz/2 cups) icing (confectioner's) sugar
> 3 tsp gum tragacanth
> 1 tsp liquid glucose
> 6 tsp cold water
> 315g (11oz) sugarpaste (rolled fondant)

1 Sieve together the icing sugar and gum tragacanth.
2 Add the liquid glucose and 6 teaspoons of cold water and mix thoroughly.
3 Knead the mixture to form soft dough, then combine this with an equal weight of sugarpaste. The paste should feel just like sugarpaste.
4 If the mixture is too dry, use a little white vegetable fat to make it soft and pliable. If the mixture is too sticky, then knead in a little sifted icing sugar.

Ganache

Ganache can be used whipped as a filling or coating, or warmed for a pour-over coating.

> 225g (8oz) dark (semisweet) chocolate, broken into small pieces
> 150ml (4½fl oz/½ cup) whipping cream

1 Put the chocolate pieces in a heatproof bowl.
2 Put the cream in a pan and heat gently until boiling.
3 Remove from the heat and pour over the chocolate.
4 Stir until the chocolate is melted and has blended into a dark mixture. Pour into a clean bowl and allow to set.
5 To pour over a cake, gently warm the ganache.
6 For piping, or filling a cake, whip until light and fluffy.

Truffles

This recipe makes approximately 16–20 truffles.

> 120g (4oz) dark (semisweet) or milk chocolate, broken into pieces
> 30ml (2 Tbsp) lightly whipped cream
> 15ml (I Tbsp) rum, brandy or sherry
> 120–150g (4–5oz/¾–1 cup) icing (confectioner's) sugar, sifted
> FOR COATING:
> White chocolate, melted
> Chocolate vermicelli
> Cocoa powder (unsweetened cocoa)

1 Melt the chocolate in a bowl, over a pan of hot water.
2 Remove the bowl from the pan and stir in the cream and alcohol.
3 Add enough sugar to form a soft paste. Cover and place in the fridge for about an hour.
4 Form into small balls. Using a fork, dip the balls into the melted white chocolate and then dip them in vermicelli or cocoa powder. Place in petit four cases.

Cake Preparation

Before you decorate your cake you need to prepare it in the correct way.

Sugarpaste (Rolled Fondant)

If you are covering a madeira cake with sugarpaste you need to coat it with a layer of buttercream or jam (jelly). If you are using a fruit cake it should first be covered with a layer of marzipan (almond paste).

How to Marzipan a Cake for Sugarpaste

A cake covered with marzipan (almond paste) needs to be left to dry for about seven days.

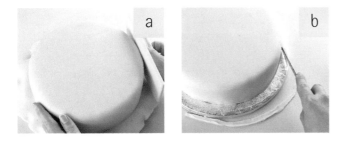

1 Place the cake on a board.

2 Spread the top and sides with warm apricot glaze.

3 Sprinkle your work surface with sieved icing sugar.

4 Knead the marzipan into a smooth ball (do not over-knead as this will bring the oils to the surface) and roll out in the shape of the cake to 5mm (¼in) thick, allowing enough for the top and sides of the cake. Make sure the marzipan moves freely, then lift gently and place evenly onto the cake.

5 Smooth the marzipan over the top and down the sides of the cake using your hands.

6 Use a cake smoother to mould the marzipan firmly to the top and sides of the cake (pic a).

7 Use a sharp knife to trim off the excess marzipan from the base of the cake, cutting down onto the board (pic b).

Covering a Cake with Sugarpaste

1 Dampen the marzipanned cake with clear alcohol.

2 Sprinkle the work surface with icing sugar. Knead the sugarpaste into a smooth ball.

3 Roll out the sugarpaste, allowing for the top and sides of the cake, and add a little extra width if you are covering the board at the same time.

4 Gently lift the sugarpaste and place it centrally on the cake.

5 Using your hands gently press the sugarpaste onto the cake, starting at the top and carefully smoothing down the sides.

6 Use a cake smoother to firmly mould the paste (pic c).

7 Trim off any excess paste at the base of the cake. If covering the cake and board in one go, smooth the icing on the board and trim off the excess around the board (pic d).

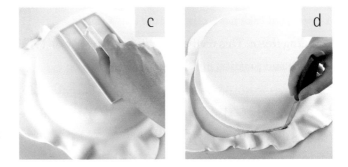

Tip

To make apricot glaze – sieve apricot jam to remove any large lumps of fruit. Heat gently until it is of a runny consistency.

Balloon Clown

A big smiling face and balloons in bright colours – just watch the children's faces as you bring in the clown.

1 Cut the cake in half horizontally and fill with jam and buttercream if desired. Place the cake centrally on the cake drum board. Cover the cake with a layer of buttercream. Colour 600g (1lb 4oz) of white sugarpaste with primrose paste colour. Cover the cake and board (see page 19).

2 To texture the board rock the

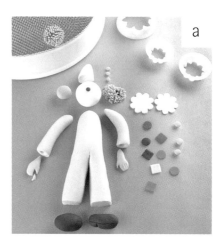

veining tool backwards and forwards over the sugarpaste.

3 Assemble the clown for the top of the cake on a non-stick mat (pic a). Body and legs – colour 160g (5½oz) of the sugarpaste with grape violet paste colour. Using 100g (3½oz), roll it into a large sausage shape – 10cm (4in) long, 4cm (1½in) wide. Make a cut half the length of the sausage to form the legs. Turn both legs inwards, tucking the cut edges down flat, leaving the rounded edges upwards. Level off the bottom of the clown's legs.

Materials

23 x 15cm (9 x 6in) octagonal
   madeira cake (see page 13)
Jam (jelly) (optional)
1 quantity buttercream (see
   page 14)
900g (2lb) white sugarpaste (rolled
   fondant)
Paste colours: primrose, grape
   violet, Christmas red, tangerine,
   black, gooseberry, mint green,
   pink, baby blue
Edible glue
Small amount of flower paste (see
   page 17)
1 heaped tsp royal icing (see
   page 15)

Equipment

Sharp knife
28 x 20cm (11 x 8in) octagonal
   cake drum board
Palette knife
Rolling pin
Cake smoother
Veining and dresden tools
Non-stick mat
Carnation cutters
Sieve
Fine paintbrush
Small round and square cutters
Clown cutter
Nos 1 and 2 piping tubes (nozzles)
Greaseproof (waxed) paper piping
   (pastry) bag
Double-sided tape
Lilac ribbon for cake drum board

4 Arms – using 30g (1¼oz) of the grape violet sugarpaste, roll it into a thin sausage 13cm (5in) long, 1.5cm (½in) wide. Cut in half. Round off the tops to form shoulders, then fix onto the body with a little edible glue. Bend the left arm over the front of the body.

5 Ruffles – roll out a little flower paste and, using the carnation cutters, cut out three large, four medium and four small. Frill the outside edges and put three large at the top of the body, two medium on the end of each leg and two small at the base of the arms, securing with a little edible glue.

6 Head – roll a 20g (¾oz) ball of white sugarpaste and carefully fix in position on the ruffles at the top of the body. Secure in place with edible glue.

7 Hat – make a cone using 10g (½oz) grape violet sugarpaste and glue into place.

8 Shoes – use 20g (¾oz) of red sugarpaste to make two small ovals. Narrow at one end to create a heel shape. Mark the bottom of each shoe with the back of a knife, forming the heel and base of the shoe. Glue into place at the end of each leg.

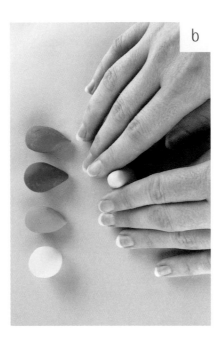

b

9 Hands – colour a little sugarpaste tangerine and make two small ovals, tapering one end to form wrists by rolling the oval between two fingers, then flatten the hands slightly. Remembering to make a left and a right hand, cut out a 'V' to form the thumb and mark the four fingers using a knife. Make a hole in the bottom of each arm using the end of a dresden tool and push the hands into place, securing with glue.

10 Nose – roll a small ball of red sugarpaste and fix into place with edible glue.

11 Pom-poms – roll three balls of primrose yellow sugarpaste and place them down the centre of the body. Roll three smaller balls and position them on the hat.

12 Hair – colour a small amount of paste using tangerine paste colour. Roll two balls of paste then press them through a sieve. Carefully remove with a knife and glue at each side of the head.

13 Paint the mouth using red paste colour and a fine paintbrush. Paint two black crosses for the eyes.

14 Roll out small pieces of sugarpaste in various colours. Cut out a few shapes (squares and circles) and place on body. Slide clown off the non-stick mat onto the cake. Secure with edible glue.

15 Make five balloons in colours of your choice (pic b). Use 10g (½oz) of sugarpaste for each balloon. Roll into a ball, then use two fingers to ease one end into a soft point. Fix the balloons in position using edible glue.

16 Now make the clowns to decorate the sides of the cake (pic c). Cut out six clowns in different sugarpaste colours using the clown cutter. Cut off the hands, feet, faces, hats and hair. Discard the faces and hands.

17 Colour a small amount of sugarpaste with tangerine and cut out six pairs of hands.

18 Roll out a little white paste and cut out six faces.

19 On the non-stick mat, re-form the clowns by mixing up all of the various coloured parts. Reverse three of them.

20 Cut out six red noses and six sets of three buttons in different colours using a no. 2 piping tube as a cutter. Fix onto the clowns. Secure the clowns in position on the side of the cake with edible glue.

21 Paint eyes and a mouth on each clown.

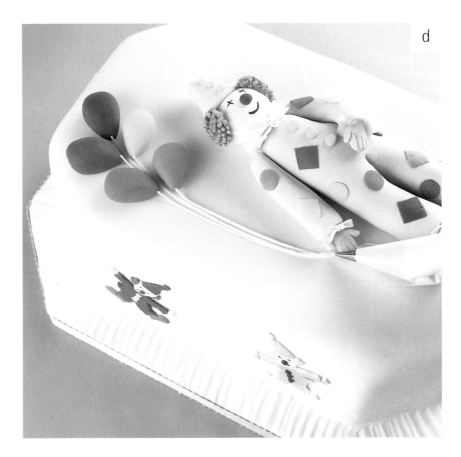

d

c

22 Put 1 heaped teaspoon of royal icing in a greaseproof paper piping bag fitted with a no. 1 piping tube. Pipe strings from the balloons to the clown's hand (pic d).

23 Stick double-sided tape around the cake drum board. Trim with lilac ribbon.

Fairy

From the land of make-believe comes this beautiful fairy with a magic wand.
A little girl would be thrilled to receive this lovely cake on her birthday.
See how easy it is to achieve such a delight.

1 Place the cake on the board. Cut in half horizontally and fill with buttercream and jam if desired.

2 Cover the whole cake with buttercream, smoothing it with a palette knife.

3 Cover the cake and board with the mint green sugarpaste (see page 19). Crimp the outside edges of the board.

4 Now make the fairy. Colour approximately 30g (1½oz) of the white sugarpaste with a small amount of chestnut brown paste colour. Divide into three – this is used for the arms, legs, body and face (pic a).

5 Use the first portion to make the legs. Roll it into a sausage shape approximately 10cm (4in) long, 7mm (¼in) in diameter. Cut in half.

6 Roll the leg between two fingers, pressing in at one end and bend at a right angle to make the foot. Pinch

Materials

20cm (8in) scalloped oval madeira
   cake (see page 13)
1 quantity buttercream (see
   page 14)
Jam (jelly) (optional)
675g (1lb 7oz) white sugarpaste
   (rolled fondant) (to be coloured
   with mint green paste colour)
125g (4½oz) white sugarpaste
   (rolled fondant)
Edible glue
Paste colours: mint green, chestnut
   brown, black, autumn leaf
Royal icing (see page 15)

Equipment

28cm (11in) scalloped oval cake drum
Sharp knife
Palette knife
Rolling pin
Cake smoother
Closed curved crimpers
Non-stick mat
Scallop and comb tool
Sunflower cutter
6-petal flower cutter
2 greaseproof (waxed) paper piping
   (pastry) bags
Nos 1 and 2 piping tubes (nozzles)
Fine paintbrush
Small blossom ejector
Yellow trellis ribbon for cake
Yellow ribbon for cake drum board

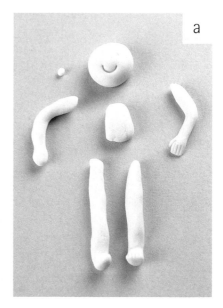

a

Skateboarding Fun

This fun cake is designed for a young boy, but it could be adapted for a girl –
maybe a girl on rollerskates or rollerblades?

a

1 Dampen your cake drum board with a little water. Roll out the light grey sugarpaste and cover the board (see page 20). Emboss with the cobblestone impression pad. Starting at the top right-hand corner, emboss all the way across (pic a). Start the next row using only half of the pad so that the pattern looks like tiles/brickwork. Continue until the whole board is embossed. Trim off any excess paste around the sides and leave to dry.

Materials

1kg (2lb 2oz) light grey sugarpaste (rolled fondant)

25 x 20cm (10 x 8in) oblong madeira cake (see page 13)

2 quantities buttercream (see page 14)

Jam (jelly) (optional)

500g (18oz) teddy bear brown sugarpaste (rolled fondant) for the cake

500g (18oz) dark grey sugarpaste

70g (2¾oz) peach sugarpaste

50g (2oz) white sugarpaste

55g (2¼oz) atlantic blue sugarpaste

20g (¾oz) teddy bear brown sugarpaste

40g (1½oz) red sugarpaste

35g (1½oz) yellow sugarpaste

20g (¾oz) black sugarpaste

Paste colours: black, mint green

Edible liquid silver

Edible glue

Royal icing (see page 15)

Equipment

30 x 45cm (12 x 18in) oblong cake drum board

Rolling pin

Sharp knife

Impression pad – cobblestone

Impression pad – brick wall

Cake smoother

Bulbous cone tool

Kemper tool

Non-stick mat

Paintbrush

Greaseproof (waxed) paper piping (pastry) bag

No. 1.5 piping tube (nozzle)

2 Cut the cake in half so you have two 12.5 x 20cm (5 x 8in) pieces of sponge (see diagram A, page 151). Place one on top of the other, then cut diagonally from the top corner of the top cake down to the bottom corner of the bottom cake (pic b and diagram B, page 151).

b

3 Assemble the pieces on the board, sandwiching them together with buttercream (and jam if desired, pic c, page 32). Buttercream the top and sides of the cake, being careful not to get buttercream on the board.

4 Roll out the teddy bear brown sugarpaste in large strips – you will need two approx. 40.5 x 15cm (16 x 6in) for the sides and two approx. 15 x 13cm (6 x 5in) for each end.

c

Emboss using the brick wall impression pad. Place onto the cake (pic d). You may find it easier to do this in sections. Trim off any excess.

5 Roll out the dark grey sugarpaste in an oblong strip (approx. 40.5 x 13cm/16 x 5in) for the top of the cake. Place in position and trim very carefully around all the sides. Smooth down using the smoother.

6 With edible liquid silver, paint two figures-of-eight on the top of the cake to represent track marks made by the skateboard.

7 Now make the boy (pic e). For the head, roll 30g (1¼oz) peach sugarpaste into a ball, approximately 4cm (1½in) in diameter. Indent the mouth using a bulbous cone tool. Roll a small ball for the nose and

stick to the face with edible glue. Place onto a non-stick mat.

8 For the ears, roll a small ball of peach sugarpaste, cut it in half and place one either side of the head at about eye level. Secure with edible glue. Indent the ears with the end of a paintbrush.

9 For the body roll 35g (1¼oz) white sugarpaste into a ball and shape into an oval. Flatten it slightly and straighten one end. Place below the head.

10 For the arms roll 20g (¾oz) peach sugarpaste into a sausage. Cut in half to make two arms. Pinch towards one end to create a hand. Cut out a 'V' for the thumb and mark in the four fingers using the tip of a knife. Make a left and right hand. Make a bend in each arm to create an elbow. Place into position.

11 For the shorts roll 35g (1¼oz) atlantic blue sugarpaste into a ball. Squash it into an oblong shape, 4 x 3cm (1½ x 1¼in). Cut a slit up the middle and open up slightly. Place onto the body.

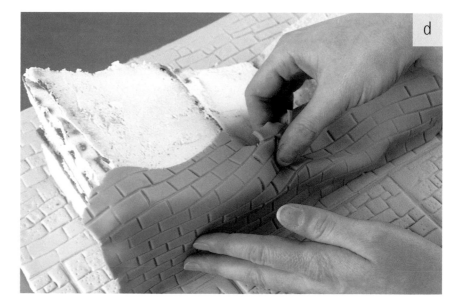

d

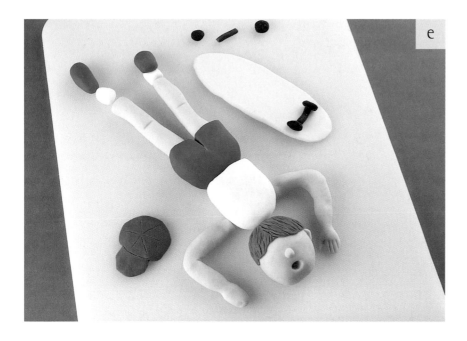

12 For the legs use 20g (¾oz) peach sugarpaste. Cut the paste in half and make two sausages 6 x 1.5cm (2¼ x ½in). Using the back of a knife, make a mark halfway down each sausage to create the back of the knee. Flatten the legs slightly and place at the bottom of the shorts.

13 Make two small balls from 5g (⅛oz) white sugarpaste, flatten slightly and push them onto the bottom of the legs for the socks.

14 For the shoes make two ovals using 10g (½oz) of atlantic blue sugarpaste. Squash and make heels with the back of a knife. Push the shoes onto the socks.

15 Make the hair using 10g (½oz) teddy bear brown sugarpaste. Make a ball and flatten it completely. Place over the top of the head, secure with edible glue, then, with a kemper tool or curved blade, texture the hair removing a small 'V' at the front and over the ears.

16 Make the cap using 10g (½oz) red sugarpaste. Roll into a ball and pinch one edge to make a brim. Mark the segments with the back of a knife. Fix onto the head.

17 Repeat step 15 to make the second cap.

18 For the boy's skateboard roll out 20g (¾oz) of yellow sugarpaste. Cut out the skateboard shape using the template on page 151. Using 5g (⅛oz) black sugarpaste roll four

small balls and flatten them. Roll two thin sausages of light grey sugarpaste to make the bars. Roll four tiny balls of white sugarpaste and secure them to the black wheels using edible glue. Secure these elements to the skateboard using edible glue.

19 For the second skateboard use 20g (¾oz) red and 5g (⅛oz) yellow sugarpaste. Roll out the red sugarpaste. Roll a thin sausage of yellow and place the sausage on top of the red sugarpaste. Roll over the paste again. Cut out a skateboard shape using the template on page 151. Make the wheels and bars as described in step 17 and attach to the skateboard using edible glue.

20 Place all the elements of the boy in position on the cake, securing with edible glue. He needs to be positioned as if he is falling off the skateboard ramp. Paint in his eyes and eyebrows using black paste colour and a fine paintbrush. Position the other elements – his skateboard, the second skateboard and the second cap. Fix all elements in position with a little royal icing.

21 Colour a small amount of royal icing mint green and put it in a piping bag fitted with a no. 1.5 piping tube. Pipe small lines up the brick wall to represent tufts of grass.

Cosmetic Purse

This is a wonderful birthday cake for a teenage girl, but it would also be suitable for Mother's Day.

1 Place the cake on the thin board, coat with warm apricot glaze and cover with marzipan (see page 19).

2 Dampen the oval cake drum board. Roll out the ivory sugarpaste and cover the drum board (see page 20). Texture using the basket weave roller. Trim off excess paste around the edge. Leave to dry.

3 Place the cake on a non-stick mat and measure the depth of the cake. Roll out lengths of peach sugarpaste and texture them using the daisy roller. Cut into strips the same width as the depth of the cake.

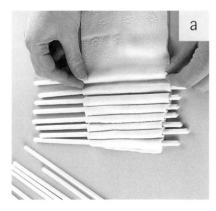

a

4 Place dowels underneath the sugarpaste strips and pinch up the paste to pleat it evenly (pic a). Remove the dowels. Press the top of the pleats together slightly, lift up and place around the sides of the cake, securing with a little water.

5 Repeat this procedure until the sides of the cake are completely covered. Make sure that all the ends are tucked in neatly.

6 Roll out a piece of peach sugarpaste slightly larger than the top of the cake. Texture using the daisy roller and cut out an oval the

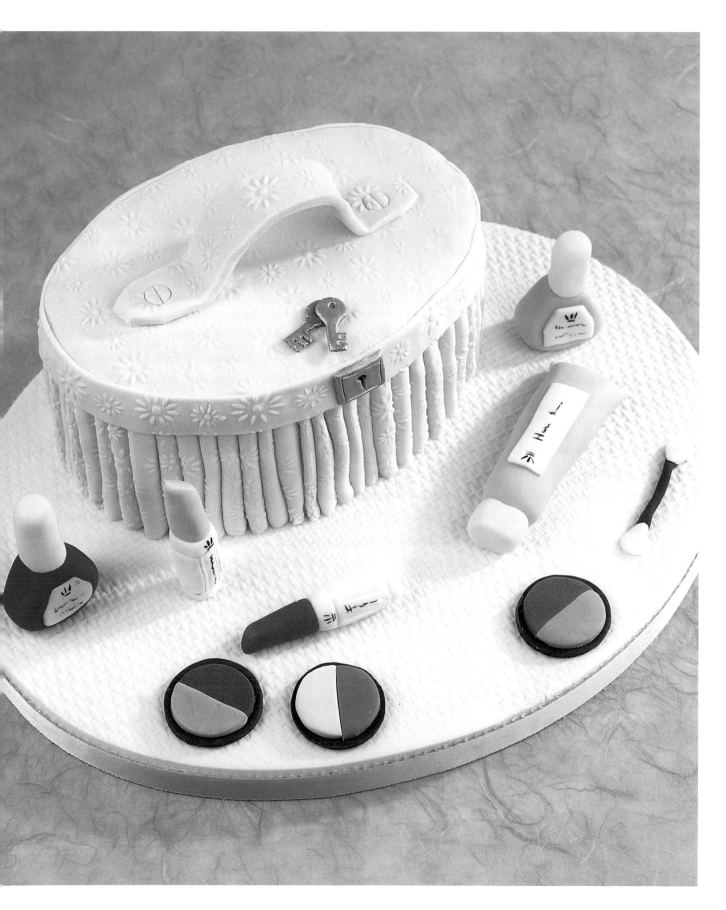

Baby's First Birthday

Cute teddy bears and brightly coloured toys and boxes will be sure to attract the baby's attention.

1 Dampen the drum board with a little water. Roll out the red sugarpaste and cover the board (see page 20). Trim off any excess sugarpaste from the edge of the board.

2 Cut the cake into the required shapes (see diagram, page 151). Cut the thin board into pieces the same size as the cakes. Place the cakes onto the appropriate board and cover with buttercream. Cover the large piece of cake with green sugarpaste.

3 Roll and cut out two strips of yellow sugarpaste, approximately 55cm (22in) long, using the small setting on the multi-ribbon cutter.

Place the strips around the top and bottom of the green box, securing with a little edible glue.

4 Roll out the white sugarpaste and, using a 5cm (2in) square cutter, cut out four squares. Place these on the sides of one of the block cakes. Cut out one 5.5cm (2¼in) square of white sugarpaste and place on top of the block (pic a). (This square needs to be bigger to cover

Tip

Mix a little clear alcohol, not water, with the food paste colours – the colours will not soak into the sugarpaste and they will dry quicker (see step 6, page 40).

Materials

15cm (6in) square sponge cake

500g (18oz) red sugarpaste (rolled fondant)

350g (12oz) green sugarpaste

55g (2½oz) yellow sugarpaste

350g (12oz) white sugarpaste

30g (1½oz) blue and pink sugarpaste

Paste colours: black, ice blue, mint green, autumn leaf, primrose, chestnut brown, pink

1 quantity buttercream (see page 14)

Edible glue

Royal icing (see page 15)

Cornflour (cornstarch)

Equipment

35 x 25cm (14 x 10in) oblong cake drum board

15cm (6in) square thin cake board

Rolling pin

Sharp knife

Multi-ribbon cutter

5cm and 5.5cm (2in and 2¼in) square cutters

Toy cutter set

Paintbrush

5 teddy bear/toy figures

Double-sided tape

Yellow ribbon for cake drum board

a

the joins on the block sides.) Repeat
this procedure for the remaining
two blocks.

5 Place the cakes onto the thin boards. Draw around the cakes and then cut the boards to the number shapes. Place the cakes onto the boards, coat with warm apricot glaze and cover with marzipan (see page 19). Place onto the covered drum board.

6 Roll out two strips of sugarpaste (choose any colour) the same width as the depth of the number 8 cake and place these inside the holes, making a neat join.

7 Roll out the six pieces of coloured sugarpaste. Use the square cutter to cut out squares in different colours (pic b).

8 Mark stitching around the outer edge of each square using the stitch wheel (pic c).

9 Emboss each coloured square with the fuchsia cutter (pic d).

10 Cover the cakes with the coloured squares (pic e), using an equal mix of colours on each cake. Push each square alongside the last one, leaving no gaps. Work around the cake in this way until it is completely covered. Some squares will have to be trimmed to fit neatly into curves and corners.

11 Place your chosen cocktail novelties into position. Stick double-sided tape around the drum board and trim with ribbon.

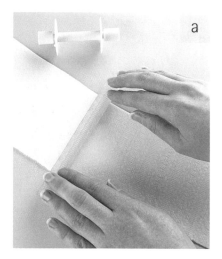

a

sugarpaste in a long strip and emboss with the floral drape roller (pic a). Use the ribbon cutter set at 4cm (1½in) to cut a strip approximately 55cm (22in) long.

6 Dust the band lightly with snow-flake lustre. Roll the band around the cake, fixing with a dab of water.

7 Roll out approximately 500g (1lb) ivory sugarpaste into a long strip, approximately 58 x 9cm (28 x 3½in) long.

5 For the hat band, roll out approximately 200g (7oz) ivory

8 Place the dowels on the work surface, so that you have three rows of two dowels set end to end. Carefully place the sugarpaste strip over the dowels and gently run your fingers up and down the sugarpaste to create three even, soft pleats (pic b).

9 Remove the dowels and carefully bring the two ends around to meet (pic c). This gives you some idea of where to position the band on the cake.

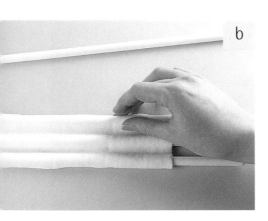

b

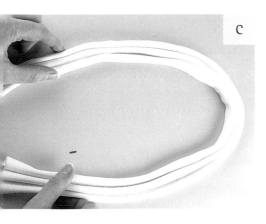

c

10 Lift the pleated paste onto the board and place in position around the cake. Pull the two ends up to meet at the top of the back of the cake. Secure with a little royal icing.

11 Using approximately 100g (4oz) of ivory sugarpaste, make the bow comprising of two loops and one knot (see steps 8–12, page 150). Fix into position where the pleats meet with a little royal icing.

12 Now make the flowers (pic d). Colour three-quarters of the remaining sugarpaste peach. Roll out and cut a strip using the ribbon cutter set at 3.5cm (1½in).

13 Fold in half lengthways, taking care not to press down on the fold. Holding the paste between the thumb and forefinger of each hand, folded edge up, roll the paste tightly a few times to form the centre of the flower. Pinch off the excess.

14 Make three separate petals, pleating the paste together into a petal shape. Place around the centre securing with a little edible glue.

15 Make a further five petals using the same method and place around the centre.

16 Make two more flowers in the same way. When the flowers are dry, dust with snowflake lustre.

17 Now make the leaves (pic d). Colour the remaining sugarpaste spruce green. Roll out the sugarpaste and using the ribbon cutter set at 3.5cm (1½in), cut out a

long strip. Cut the strip into 5cm (2in) lengths.

18 Place cocktail sticks alternately above and below the pieces of sugarpaste. Pinch together to ease the sugarpaste into forming pleats.

19 Remove the sticks and pinch the paste at each end. Pinch off any excess to emphasize the points and to create a leaf shape.

20 Make three more leaves in the same way. When dry, dust with snowflake lustre.

21 Referring to the photograph on page 48, assemble the leaves and flowers as shown, securing with a little royal icing. Add feathers if desired.

22 Stick double-sided tape around the cake drum board and trim with ribbon.

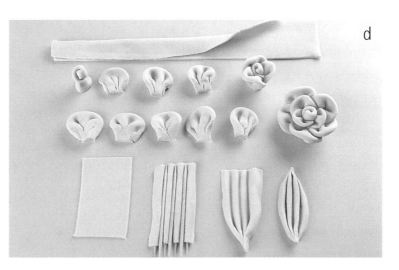

d

b

c

7 Now make the small bows. Roll out a strip of sugarpaste approximately 3mm (⅛in) thick. Texture the paste in the same way as you did for the swag (see step 2, page 50).

8 Cut out six small pieces of the textured sugarpaste, approximately 6.5 x 1cm (2½ x ¾in) and turn each one over (pic b). Take one of the sugarpaste pieces and fold the ends into the centre. Turn over to hide the seam and, with the tweezers, indent to create the centre knot of the bow (as shown in pic b). Pinch either side of the knot to create a bow shape. Place onto the cake at each swag end, securing with a little royal icing.

9 Using a No. 3 piping tube, pipe four balls of royal icing below the bow to cover the swag seams (pic c).

10 Roll out the remaining white sugarpaste and carefully cut out the numbers required using a knife or cutting wheel.

11 Divide the white sugarpaste you have left into four and colour with the paste colours listed on page 50. Roll out and cut out a selection of small blossoms and hearts.

12 Cover the numbers in the heart and blossom shapes, securing them with a little edible glue (pic d).

13 Place a line of assorted coloured blossoms around the base of the cake, on the board. Stick double-sided tape around the edge of the drum board and trim with the white ribbon.

d

80th Birthday

I have used ready-made grape sprays on this cake. Make the plaque in advance so that it dries thoroughly.

a

Materials

20cm (8in) round rich fruit cake (see page 12)

125g (4½oz) modelling paste (see page 18)

Paste colours: cream, bordeaux, gooseberry green

Cornflour (cornstarch)

Apricot glaze

Marzipan (almond paste) (see page 17) (quantity should be equal to half weight of cake)

450g (1lb) royal icing (see page 15)

700g (1½lb) ivory sugarpaste (rolled fondant)

25g (1oz) flower paste (see page 17)

5 ready-made grape sprays

Equipment

20cm (8in) round, thin cake board

35cm (14in) round cake drum board

Rolling pin

Long octagonal plaque cutter, 14 x 10cm (5½ x 4in)

Straight-edge

Side scraper

Sharp knife

Veining tool

Abutilon/speckled leaf cutters

Double-sided tape

Olive green ribbon for cake drum board

1 Colour the modelling paste cream. Roll out and cut out a long octagonal plaque using the cutter (pic a).

2 Using the template on page 151, cut out the triangle shape for the backrest for the plaque.

3 Place the plaque and backrest onto a flat board dusted with cornflour. Place to one side and allow to dry completely.

4 Place the cake on the thin board. Coat with apricot glaze and cover with marzipan (see page 20).

5 Colour the royal icing with cream paste colour. Be cautious and add only a little colour at a time. The icing will darken as it stands, so you do need to take care not to over-colour. Mix thoroughly and allow to stand.

6 Cover the cake with the cream royal icing (see page 21).

7 Roll out the ivory sugarpaste and cover the cake drum board (see page 20).

8 Carefully place the cake into the centre of the covered drum board and with a veining tool, texture all the way around the cake, rocking the tool backwards and forwards (pic b).

9 Divide the flower paste into two. Colour one half with bordeaux and the other with gooseberry green.

10 Roll out the green petal paste and cut out leaves using the smallest cutter from the set. Cut out 10. Then, cut out four large leaves. Using gooseberry green paste colour, paint veins on all the leaves.

11 Arrange the leaves around the plaque (pic c). Cut two of the small leaves in half and place at the bottom of the plaque. Position two of the large leaves at the top in the centre and one midway down each side. Secure with edible glue. Paint a vine on the plaque to join the leaves with gooseberry green paste colour.

12 The number 80 is formed using bunches of grapes. Roll tiny balls of bordeaux coloured flower paste and group them together to form bunches (roughly triangle shaped). You will need approximately 22 bunches. Form the 80 on the plaque (pic d), and once you're happy with the arrangement, secure into position with a little edible glue.

13 Place the plaque face down on a piece of foam. Place the backrest in the centre of the reverse side of the plaque and secure with royal icing (pic e). Allow the royal icing to dry completely.

14 Position the grape sprays around the base of the cake and secure to the drum board with a little royal icing.

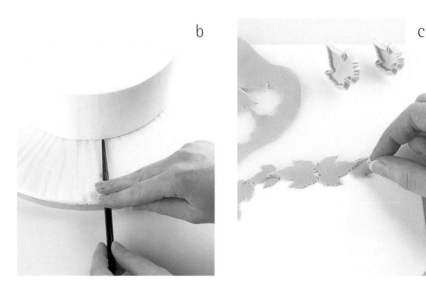

b

c

d

e

15 Sit the plaque in the centre of the cake and secure with royal icing if necessary.

16 Stick double-sided tape around the edge of the drum board and trim with ribbon.

Engagement Ring Box

What lady wouldn't like to be given a beautiful solitaire in such a pretty box? This cake will make it a day to remember.

1 Draw around the hexagonal double thick cake board onto a piece of greaseproof paper. Cut out and use as a template for the box lid in step 4.

2 Roll out the ivory sugarpaste and cover the round drum board (see page 20). Crimp the edges using closed triple scallop crimpers.

3 Place the cake, rounded side up, onto the double thick board. Coat the cake with apricot glaze and cover with marzipan (see page 19).

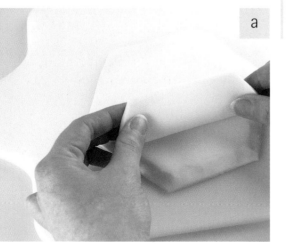

a

4 To make the lid colour 125g (4¼oz) modelling paste with cream paste colour. Use the template made in step 1 to cut out a hexagon. Repeat, except this time colour the paste with grape violet paste colour. Place the hexagons one on top of the other and leave to dry.

5 To create the cushioned effect of the top of the box, form a thick hexagonal pad of ivory sugarpaste. Cover with a thin layer of ivory sugarpaste (pic a) and then place on top of the cake. Secure with a little water.

b

water and then carefully wrap the strip around the cake (pic b).

7 Using a sugarcraft gun fitted with the half circle disc, push out a long strip of lilac sugarpaste and fix it around five sides of the hexagonal lid with a little water (pic c).

8 Place the lid into position on the box, securing with royal icing. You will need to support the lid whilst it is drying.

9 Make another half circle strip (see step 7) to go around the top edge of the cake and over the lid

6 Colour the white sugarpaste with the grape violet paste colour. Roll out a strip long enough to fit around the cake (approximately 7.5 x 50cm/3 x 20in) and emboss it with the quilting embosser. Dampen the cake with clear alcohol or boiled

> *Tip*
> Measurements given for hexagonal tins are from point to point. Boards are from flat to flat. This is how they are sold, so double-check when buying.

join at the back of the cake. Secure with a little water.

10 Place dragees where the pattern lines intersect on the sides of the cake. Secure with royal icing (pic d).

11 To make the ring roll a 7.5cm (3in) long sausage of modelling paste, about 1.5cm (½in) thick. Bend in half to form a half ring shape. Cut the ends at an angle so that they will stand level on the cake.

12 Fix your chosen solitaire decoration onto the ring using royal icing (pic e) and allow to dry.

13 Paint the ring with edible liquid gold and leave to dry. Position on the cake securing with royal icing.

14 Stick double-sided tape around the edge of the drum board and trim with ribbon.

c

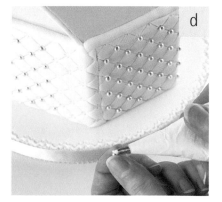

d

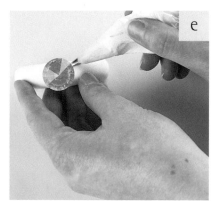

e

Three-tier
Rose
Wedding Cake

This cake looks spectacular, but is easy to create. I have decorated this cake using ready-made roses, but if you want to make your own see the tip on page 61.

Materials

3 hexagonal rich fruit cakes (see page 12) measuring from point to point: 15cm (6in), 23cm (9in), 30cm (12in)

Apricot glaze

2.5kg (5lb 10oz) marzipan (almond paste) (see page 17)

2.75kg (6lb 2oz) ivory sugarpaste (rolled fondant)

Royal icing (see page 15)

Cream paste colour

26 ready-made large roses

11 ready-made small roses

Small amount of flower paste (see page 17) coloured cream using paste colour

Edible glue

Snowflake lustre

Equipment

3 hexagonal cake drum boards,
measuring from flat to flat:
15cm (6in), 23cm (9in), 30cm (12in)

Rolling pin

Sharp knife

Cake smoother

Single closed curve crimpers

1 circular dummy 6cm (2½in) wide x 5cm (2in) deep

1 circular dummy 10cm (4in) wide x 5cm (2in) deep

Greaseproof (waxed) paper

Small piping (pastry) bag

No. 2 piping tube (nozzle)

24-gauge white wires

26-gauge silver wires

Small plastic favour dish

Golf ball-sized ball of Stay Soft (like white Plasticine™)

Small heart cutter

Double-sided tape

Ivory ribbon for cake drum boards

1 Place each of the cakes onto the appropriate drum board. Coat the cakes with apricot glaze and cover with marzipan (see page 19). Cover the cakes and drum boards with ivory sugarpaste (see page 19). Save any trimmings for covering the dummies in step 3.

2 Crimp the outside edge of the pasted boards with crimpers.

3 Roll out a long strip of ivory sugarpaste 5cm (2in) wide and wrap around the sides of the two dummies, fixing in position with a little water.

4 Cut two circles of greaseproof paper, the size of each dummy. Place the largest circle of greaseproof paper in the centre of the largest cake and then place the larger dummy on top. Fix all of the

completely. Dust each heart with snowflake lustre.

9 Twist the wires then arrange them in the top tier decoration (pic d).

10 Stick double-sided tape around the edge of each drum board and trim with ribbon. Assemble the cake. When stacking the cakes, make sure that each one is placed centrally for balance. Place the arrangement on the top tier, securing with a little royal icing.

elements in place with a little royal icing. Repeat for the middle tier.

5 Colour some royal icing with cream paste colour to match the sugarpaste and place in a small piping bag fitted with a no. 2 piping tube. Pipe balls randomly on each cake tier (pic a). Concentrate them around the bottom of each cake and then scatter a few up the sides so that they look like fizzing bubbles.

6 Arrange the large roses around the dummies on the bottom and middle tier (reserve four for the top tier) (pic b). Once you are happy, fix in place with a little royal icing.

7 For the top tier decoration, wire

the small roses and four large roses. Do this by fixing a 24-gauge wire to the back of each rose with royal icing. (Most ready-made roses have a hole in the back of the flower which makes it easy to attach the wire.) Arrange them on the favour dish containing Stay Soft. First put one large rose in the centre, then put the remaining three large roses around it. Fill with the smaller roses until you have a pleasing dome effect.

8 To create the small hearts for the top tier decoration, roll out the cream petal paste. Cut out a number of hearts. Thread two onto each 26-gauge wire, one part way down and the other at the end (pic c). Secure with a little edible glue. Allow to dry

Tip

To make your own roses refer to steps 7–16, pages 83–84 for the basics. For this cake you will need to make the roses from flower paste (see page 17). Make 22 large roses, 11 small wired roses and 4 larger wired roses. For the wired roses you will need to make cone shapes. Insert a 24-gauge hooked wire into each cone and allow to dry. Place petals around the cone to form the rose.

Chocolate
Wedding Cake

Chocoholics will love this cake with its combination of white and dark chocolate.
It's easy to make as the chocolate triangles and curls are ready-made.

1 Cut each cake in half horizontally and fill with jam if desired. Fix the largest cake centrally onto the drum board with buttercream. Fix the two other tiers to the appropriate boards in the same way.

2 The cakes need to be supported with dowels. Insert a dowel into the bottom tier and make a mark on the dowel level with the top of the cake. Remove the dowel and cut it where you made the mark. Cut three more pieces of dowel to the same length.

Tip
To stop the white chocolate curls melting in your hand, make a cone out of greaseproof paper, fill with the curls and then sprinkle them on the cake.

Materials
3 triangular chocolate cakes,
   30cm (12in), 25cm (10in),
   20cm (8in) (see page 12)
5 quantities buttercream (see
   page 14)
Jam (jelly) (optional)
150 ready-made chocolate triangles,
   plus extra to allow for breakages
500g (18oz) ready-made white
   chocolate curls
50g (2oz) white Belgian chocolate
100g (3½oz) dark (semisweet)
   Belgian chocolate

Equipment
45cm (18 in) triangular cake drum

board (flat edge)
2 triangular thin cake boards, 20cm
   (8in), 25cm (10in)
8 dowels
Palette knife
Side scraper
Sharp knife
Acetate
Cotton wool
Marble slab or similar
Heatproof bowl
Saucepan
Teaspoon
Mug or similar
Non-stick mat
Double-sided tape
Cream ribbon for cake drum

Insert in the bottom tier – one close to each point of the triangle and one in the centre. Repeat for the middle tier. Stack the cakes making sure each one is central.

3 Spread buttercream over the cakes and the top of the drum board using a palette knife, be as neat as you can. Tidy up the buttercream with a side scraper.

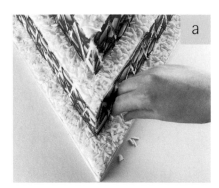

4 Starting with the bottom tier, place a row of the chocolate triangles along the base on all three sides. The shortest edge of the triangle should align with the base of the cake. Press them in gently, leaving an equal amount of space in between. At the corners you will have to split the triangles in half. To do this cut with a warm knife.

5 To complete the bottom tier, place a second row of triangles in between the row that is already on the cake. This time the shortest edge of the triangle should align with the top of the bottom tier. Repeat for the other two tiers.

6 Scatter the white chocolate curls around the drum and on the top of each tier (pic a).

7 Using the templates on page 152, trace eight bow loops and three tails onto acetate. Use cotton wool to polish the acetate to remove any fingermarks or grease. Place the acetate pieces onto a marble slab.

8 Break the white chocolate into pieces and place in a heatproof bowl. Melt over a saucepan of hot water, making sure that neither water or steam comes into contact with the chocolate.

9 Dribble the white chocolate randomly over all of the acetate pieces. Allow to set for a few minutes whilst you melt the dark chocolate (see step 8 above).

10 Using a teaspoon, spread the dark chocolate over the top of the white, completely covering the acetate shapes (pic b). Leave for 1 minute, then pick up each bow piece and smooth off the outer edges with your fingers. Curl the loop pieces over to make a loop. Pinch the two ends together. Place the end of each loop underneath a mug (or something similar) whilst setting.

Tip
The bow should be made the day before the wedding as untempered chocolate can bloom. To prevent this happening, try coating the bow in confectioners' varnish.

11 When completely set gently peel off the acetate. Place the three tails centrally on the top tier. Assemble the bow on a non-stick mat (pic c). Secure with a little melted chocolate.

12 Allow the bow to set completely and place on top of the cake, securing it with a little melted chocolate.

13 Stick double-sided tape around the edge of the drum board and trim with ribbon.

Daisy
Wedding Cake

This bright, summery cake with individual muffins is a modern variation of the traditional three-tier wedding cake.

1 Place a small amount of the pink paste colour into the buttercream, mixing thoroughly. Leave to stand to allow the colour to develop. Mix again before use.

2 Insert the piping tube into the large piping bag and half fill with pink buttercream.

3 Starting with the large cake, pipe from the outer edge to the centre of the cake. Continue doing this until the top of the cake is covered. Turn the cake after you've piped a few rows to create a curved, wave effect.

Materials

18cm (7in) round madeira cake (see page 13)
36 muffin cakes (make mixture for a 23cm (9in) madeira cake; put 1 dessertspoonful of mixture in each case, bake for 30 minutes at 160°C/325°F/Gas mark 3
Pink paste colour
5 quantities buttercream (see page 14)
Flower paste (see page 17)
Edible glue

Equipment

3-tier cake stand
36 silver paper muffin cases
Large piping (pastry) bag
No. 13 piping tube (nozzle)
45 small and 6 large sugar daisies
18g green wires
White floristry tape
Posy pick
Wide silver ribbon for top tier cake

small daisies and one large daisy, varying the length of wire from flower to flower. Secure with a small ball of flower paste and a little edible glue (pic c). Allow to dry.

7 Place a posy pick into the centre of the large cake.

8 Arrange the wired daisies as if they are growing out of the top of the cake. Then arrange five large daisies around the cake. (You may need to secure them with a little buttercream, pic d.)

9 Place a silver ribbon around the large cake and place onto the top tier of the stand.

10 Arrange the muffins on the two lower tiers of the stand.

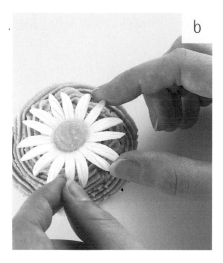

4 Pipe buttercream on the muffins. Start at the outside edge of the cake and swirl up and around to the centre (pic a).

5 Allow the buttercream swirls to dry a little before placing a small sugar daisy on the top of each cake (pic b).

6 Cut varying lengths of wire. Cover with white tape. Place a wire onto the back of the remaining

Wedding Gifts

This bride and groom just couldn't wait to open their gifts. If you need more cake, simply make more parcels.

1 Roll out the white sugarpaste and cover the drum board (see page 20). Emboss the sugarpaste with a textured rolling pin and trim off any excess paste. Leave to dry.

2 Cut the madeira cakes into pieces for the parcels, using the diagrams on page 152. I recommend that you make a template out of greaseproof paper for each one and label with the relevant parcel number. Use this template to cut the thin board for the base of each parcel also.

3 Cut thin boards for the bottom of each parcel. Secure cakes to the boards with buttercream. Coat the sponge pieces in buttercream as you go along, before covering with sugarpaste.

4 Refer to the diagram opposite when making the parcels. Parcels 1 and 2 – cover with white sugarpaste then emboss all over using the blossom cutter.

Materials

2 x 20cm (8in) square madeira cakes, 7cm (3in) deep

1kg (2lb 2oz) white sugarpaste (rolled fondant) (for drum board)

2 quantities buttercream (see page 14)

Paste colours: chestnut brown, autumn leaf, spruce green, black

Royal icing (see page 15)

For parcels:

550g (1lb 4oz) white sugarpaste

575g (1lb 5oz) lilac sugarpaste

400g (14oz) pink sugarpaste

300g (11oz) shell pink sugarpaste

For the bride and groom:

20g (¾oz) black sugarpaste

90g (3¼oz) peach sugarpaste

20g (¾oz) dark grey sugarpaste

30g (1½oz) white sugarpaste

10g (½oz) flower paste (see page 17)

Equipment

45 x 30cm (18 x 12in) oblong cake drum board

Thin cake boards (enough for bases for all parcels)

Rolling pin

Cake smoother

Fabric texture roller

Sharp knife

Greaseproof (waxed) paper

Palette knife

Blossom plunger cutter

7cm (2¾in) square cutter

Heart plunger cutter

Decorative cutter motifs

Cone tool

Kemper tool

Ivy leaf cutter

Pink ribbon

Fine paintbrush

7 small silver bows

Double-sided tape

White ribbon for cake drum board

5 Parcel 3 – wrap the sides with lilac sugarpaste (pic a). Make a lid of lilac sugarpaste using the square cutter and place it on the top of the box. Ease the paste around the corners and trim if necessary.

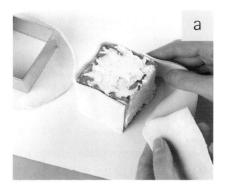

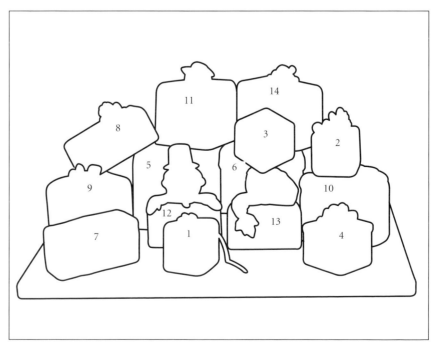

12 Now make the decoration for the ring cake. To make the spirals, hold the wire between the pliers and twist the wire around once. Now hold this flat between your fingers and continue to curl the wire around to make a spiral.

13 Take another length of wire, but this time make a sprial at each end. Bend the wire in half. Attach to the single spiral by twisting the wires together. Now twist the spirals to the base of a lily (pic c). Repeat for the other eight lilies.

14 Place the lilies evenly around the ring cake securing with a little royal icing. Gently ease the spirals downwards so that they 'fall' over the cake.

15 Place a posy pick into the centre of the round cake. Trim the base of the cake with silver threaded beads.

16 Make 10 more spirals – five short and five long – and place them into the posy pick. Spread them evenly around the top of the cake and gently ease the spirals downwards so that they 'fall' over the cake.

17 Make 10 more spirals in an assortment of lengths. Twist together with three lilies and place

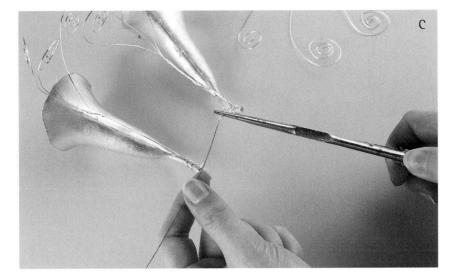

into the posy pick. Make any necessary adjustments to make a pleasing arrangement (pic d).

18 Place sprigs of silver beads randomly in the arrangement. Finish by filling any gaps around the posy pick with silver dragees secured with royal icing.

19 Stick double-sided tape around the edge of the drum boards and trim with ribbon.

Pearl Wedding
Anniversary

What couple wouldn't love to receive this delightful cake with its shimmering pearls to celebrate 30 years of marriage?

Materials

20cm (8in) and 30cm (12in) teardrop-shaped rich fruit cakes (see page 12)

700g (1½lb) white sugarpaste (rolled fondant) (for the drum board)

1kg (2lb 2oz) white sugarpaste (rolled fondant) (for large cake)

500g (18oz) white sugarpaste (rolled fondant) (for small cake)

Apricot glaze

1½kg (3lb 5oz) marzipan (almond paste) (see page 17)

250g (9oz) modelling paste (see page 18)

Cornflour (cornstarch)

Silver snowflake lustre

Petal base

Royal icing (see page 15)

Equipment

38cm (15in) oval cake drum board

2 thin cake boards, cut to shape of cakes

Rolling pin

Sharp knife

Cake smoother

Fabric textured roller

Scalloped crimpers

Half-ball set (including extra large ball)

8mm (⅜in) bead cutter

Small paintbrush

Double-sided tape

White ribbon for cake drum board

1 Roll out the white sugarpaste for the drum board. Dampen the board with a little water and cover with the sugarpaste (see page 20). Texture using the fabric textured roller and trim off the excess paste. Crimp the outer edges using scalloped crimpers.

2 Place each cake onto the thin boards, turning the smaller cake over so that when stacked it sits the opposite way to the larger cake.

3 Coat the cakes with apricot glaze and cover with marzipan (see page 19). Roll out the white sugarpaste for the large cake and cover (see page 19). Smooth down the sides and trim loosely. Repeat to give a clean edge. Add the trimmings to the quantity of sugarpaste for the small cake and cover the small cake.

4 Place the large cake onto the covered board and the smaller cake on top (refer to photo above). Fill in any gaps with a little royal icing (pic a), smoothing the joins with your little finger. Leave the cake to dry.

5 To make the pearls, roll balls of modelling paste and dust them lightly with cornflour. Starting with the extra large mould, press the

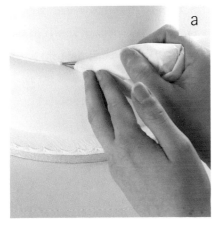

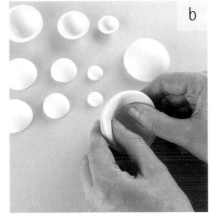

paste into the mould (pic b). Keep the paste moving and repeatedly take the paste out and re-dust it with cornflour. When you are satisfied with the half-ball shape, trim off the excess paste, turn out on a flat surface and leave to dry. Make the following half-balls; 8 extra large, 4 large, 10 medium, and 8 small.

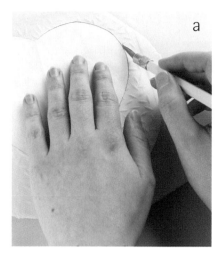

a

5 Roll out the sugarpaste and texture using the rice-textured roller. Cut out the heart-shaped cushion cover using the template on page 153 (pic a).

6 Gently place the cushion cover over the top of the cushion. Trim and shape the cushion if necessary so that the two fit together neatly. Remove the cushion cover temporarily.

7 Dampen the top of the cushion inner and put the cushion cover in place (pic b).

8 Using a sugarcraft gun fitted with the ridged ribbon disc, slowly press out the sugarpaste and place around the outer edge of the cushion, securing with a little water (pic c).

9 Dampen the top of the cake and place the heart-shaped cushion in the centre.

10 Dampen the oval drum board with a little water. Roll out the sugarpaste and cover the board. Texture using the rice-textured roller. Trim off any excess paste around the edges. Leave the board to dry.

11 Place the stand centrally, towards the back of the oval drum board. Put the favour dish containing Stay Soft at the front of the drum and arrange the silk

flowers (pic d). You may need to tape some of the flowers together with green floristry tape to keep them in the right position.

12 Stick double-sided tape around the edge of the drum boards and trim with ribbon.

13 Place the cake on the stand and put the ring and dove decoration on the cushion. Secure in position with a little royal icing.

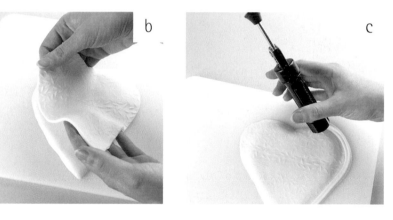

b

c

d

Golden Wedding
Anniversary

This quick and easy cake can be made and decorated on the same day. You can freeze the buttercreamed cake, but do not freeze the rose decoration.

Materials

23cm (9in) heart-shaped madeira or chocolate cake (see pages 12 and 13)
Jam (jelly) or ganache (see page 18)
I quantity buttercream (see page 14)
I quantity buttercream (see page 14) coloured with autumn leaf paste colour
100g (3½oz) marzipan (almond paste) (see page 17)
Paste colours: autumn leaf, spruce green

Equipment

30cm (12in) round gold cake drum board
2 no. 44 piping tubes (nozzles)
2 large piping (pastry) bags
Rose leaf cutter and veiner (large and medium)
Double-sided tape
Gold ribbon for cake drum board

1 Cut the cake in half horizontally and fill with jam and buttercream (for madeira cake) or ganache (for chocolate cake). Fix into place on the drum board with a little buttercream.

2 Fit the piping tubes into the piping bags. Fill one piping bag with the buttercream and the other with the autumn leaf buttercream.

3 Starting at the base of the cake, pipe a line of buttercream stars all the way around.

4 Change bags and pipe a line of stars above the previous line. Continue to pipe alternate coloured lines until you reach the centre of the cake (pic a).

5 Finish the centre with a few of the appropriate coloured stars. Place the cake to one side in a cool place to set.

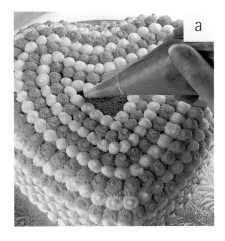
a

6 To make the marzipan roses, colour three-quarters of the marzipan with autumn leaf paste colour. You need to make one rosebud and two larger roses (pic b, page 84).

7 For the rosebud, make a long cone with some of the marzipan and roll it gently between your fingers, moving your fingers up and down, to form a pointed bud shape.

8 Roll five balls of marzipan, each should be about the size of a large pea. Press out each one to make a petal shape, leaving the marzipan a little thicker at one edge.

Tip

To make the petals, place the balls of marzipan inside a polythene bag and then press them into a petal shape. This prevents the marzipan sticking to your fingers.

9 Wrap the first petal right around the cone, overlapping the edge. Squeeze the base gently to secure.

10 Place the second petal directly over the seam of the first, wrapping it right around.

11 Attach one side of the third petal firmly and leave the other side free; turn the very edge of the petal back slightly.

12 Place the centre of the fourth petal over the closed side of the third and attach to the cone, curling back the edge.

13 Place the centre of the fifth petal over the edge of the fourth and under the open side of the third, and close the edge of the third petal down. Curl the edges of the fifth petal. This completes the rosebud.

14 To make a bigger rose, make a rosebud and add around five slightly larger petals, keeping them all a similar height. Remember to stretch each petal around the base as you secure, and apply each petal so that it overlaps the previous one about halfway and curl the edges outwards.

15 When the rose is the required shape and size, gently press down each of the petals to ensure they are secure.

16 Cut the bases of the roses and bud so that they will sit flat on the cake. Leave to dry.

17 For the leaves, colour the remaining marzipan spruce green; roll it out. Using the large and medium rose leaf cutters and veiners, cut and press out approximately six large leaves and three medium ones.

18 Twist each leaf a little to show movement and leave to dry.

19 Place the roses and leaves onto the cake (pic c). Secure with a little buttercream.

20 Stick double-sided tape around the edge of the drum board and trim with ribbon.

b

c

Diamond Wedding
Anniversary

What could be more fitting to celebrate 60 years of marriage than this diamond-shaped cake? I've given it sparkle with edible glitter.

1 Put the cake on the drum board. Coat the cake with apricot glaze and cover with marzipan (see page 20). Cover the cake and board with royal icing (see page 21).

2 Roll out the flower paste to about 3mm (⅛in) thick. Use the hollow oval cutter to cut out ovals. You will need approximately 38, but make a few extra to allow for breakages. Place them over a rolling pin (or

Materials

20cm (8in) (measured at flat edge) diamond-shaped rich fruit cake (see page 12)

Marzipan (almond paste) (half weight of cake) (see page 17)

450–700g (1–1½lb) royal icing (see page 15)

175g (6oz) flower paste (see page 17)

Edible glue

Edible silver glitter

Equipment

Rolling pin

Sharp knife

Palette knife

Side scraper

Straight edge

32cm (12½in) (measured at flat edge) diamond-shaped cake drum board

Lace leaf cutters

Lace flower cutters

Hollow oval cutter

24-gauge white wires

White floristry tape

Veining board

Lilac ribbon for cake drum board

Double-sided tape

Pliers

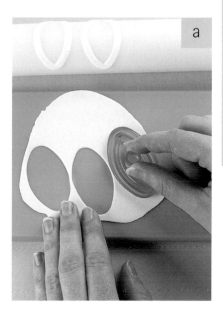

a

tube of some kind) to dry (pic a). They will dry into an arched shape.

3 For the flower centres roll 5mm (¼in) balls of flower paste. Flatten

them to 1cm (½in) rounds. Make a ski pole with 24-gauge wire by holding the wire end with pliers and curling the wire around. Put some edible glue onto the ball of flower

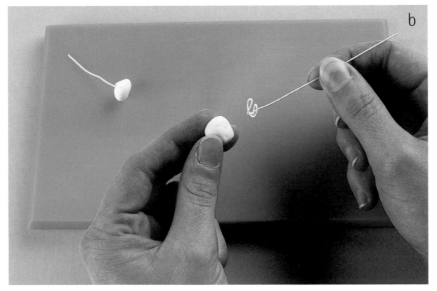

paste and press the pole in it (pic b). Allow to dry completely.

4 Roll out the flower paste and cut out five large and five smaller flowers using the lace flower cutters. The flowers need to be put into something curved to dry – I've used the cups from an apple tray (the kind you see in supermarkets). Place the larger flowers in the cups (pic c). Place the smaller flowers on top of the larger ones so that the petals go

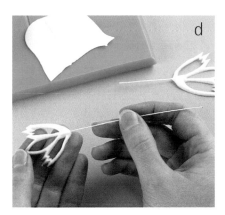

in between the larger ones. Pierce a hole through the centre of the flowers and place the centre into position securing with a little edible glue. Leave to dry completely.

5 Roll out the flower paste on a veining board. Cut out eight larger and eight smaller leaves using the lace leaf cutters. Cut 16 10cm (4in) lengths of 24-gauge wire. Insert a wire into the base of each leaf where the groove is (pic d). Leave to dry on small pieces of foam, propping up some of the edges so

that when they dry the leaves will have some shape to them. This gives the arrangement more life.

6 When all of the decorative elements are completely dry, coat the top surface of the ovals with edible glue, dip them into edible glitter, shake off the excess and place carefully to dry. Repeat this procedure with the leaves and flowers.

7 Starting at the front point of the cake, place the ovals evenly around the cake. Overlap each one, bringing one forward and one back alternately, securing into position with a little royal icing. Repeat all the way along the flat sides, placing an extra oval at the points at the top and bottom of the diamond.

8 To wire the leaves start with a large leaf. Take the white floristry

tape and wrap the wire until you are about halfway down. Add two smaller leaves, one on each side and continue to tape down the wire. Make four of these groups of leaves.

9 Tape the wires of the remaining leaves and flowers.

10 Place a ball of flower paste into the middle of the cake and fix with a little royal icing.

11 Start arranging the top decoration into a diamond shape by placing one leaf group towards each point of the cake, making the two side points a little shorter. Place the remaining leaves in between.

12 Place one flower at each point and balance one on top in the centre.

13 Stick double-sided tape around the edge of the drum board and trim with ribbon.

> **Tip**
> It is best to do any of the tasks involving glitter away from your preparation surfaces as it tends to spread everywhere!

b

to match up where the lines meet at the edge of each section as this will make for a neater pattern.

8 Roll out the atlantic blue sugarpaste and place onto a dusted non-stick mat.

9 Trace the template on page 154 onto greaseproof paper. Place the template on top of the sugarpaste, pencil side facing upwards. Use a

craft knife to carefully trace over the outline of the template, applying light pressure so that it marks the sugarpaste beneath (pic b).

10 Remove the template and use a cutting wheel to cut around the outline of the shape. Carefully remove the centre cut-outs with a sharp knife (pic c).

11 Lift the non-stick mat to the cake and gently slide the sugarpaste star into the centre of the cake (pic d).

12 Stick double-sided tape around the edge of the drum board and trim with ribbon.

c

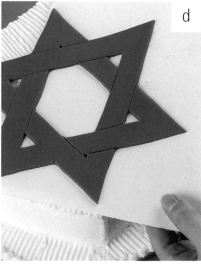
d

Simnel Cake

A Simnel cake was a traditional offering given by servant girls to their mothers on the fourth Sunday in Lent, which has now become Mothering Sunday. Simnel cakes are now also eaten at Easter, when 11 balls of marzipan are placed on top of the cake to represent the 11 true apostles.

Materials

Mixture for a 20cm (8in) rich fruit cake (see page 12 and step 1 right)

225g (½lb) marzipan (almond paste) (for baking) (see page 17)

500g (1lb 2oz) marzipan (almond paste) (for top and decoration) (see page 17)

Apricot glaze

Equipment

25cm (10in) round gold cake drum

Rolling pin

Sharp knife

Closed curve serrated crimpers

Straight edge

Easter duck or chick decorations

Broad yellow ribbon

Double-sided tape

Gold paper ribbon

1 Place half of the rich fruit cake mixture into the tin and level the surface. Using 225g (8oz) of marzipan, roll it into a circle the same size as the tin. Place it on top of the mixture. Spoon the remaining mixture over the top and smooth the surface. Bake as directed (see page 12).

2 It is not necessary to turn the cake upside down as traditionally the top has a rounded edge. If, however, your cake has a slight hollow in the top, fill it in with marzipan brushed with warm apricot glaze (pic a).

3 Roll out the marzipan. Place the cake tin in which the cake was baked onto the marzipan and cut around it. Cover the top of the cake with warm apricot glaze and place the circle of marzipan on it.

a

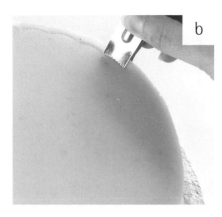

4 Crimp around the edge of the marzipan (pic b).

5 Using a straight edge and a sharp knife, lightly score a diamond pattern onto the surface of the marzipan (pic c).

6 Roll 11 equal-sized balls of marzipan and place around the outside edge of the top of the cake (pic d). Space the balls evenly. Secure with a little dab of water.

7 Put the cake under the grill for a few minutes to brown the top. Keep a close eye on it, don't let it burn!

8 Set the cake on the cake drum board. Place the duck or chick decorations in the centre of the cake. Attach the yellow ribbon around the cake, then put the gold paper ribbon around the middle. Secure with double-sided tape.

6 Cover the assembled cake with chocolate buttercream using a palette knife. Texture the surface with a fork (pic b).

7 Spread royal icing over the board and pat the icing with a palette knife to form peaks (pic c).

8 To make the robins (pic d): weigh out 40g (1½oz) modelling paste and divide into two equal pieces.

Roll each piece into a large cone shape. Shape the head to form the beak. Pinch the bottom part of the bird where the tail will go into a point. Using a craft knife, score all over to give the appearance of a feathered texture.

to the front and one to the back. Push the legs into the body. Leave both birds to dry.

9 Indent a hole for both eyes. Roll out the remaining modelling paste and cut out the wings and tails using the templates on page 154. With a dresden tool, mark in the feathers. Place onto the bird's body, securing with a little royal icing.

10 Now make the legs. Cut 16 2cm (⅜in) lengths of 24-gauge wire. Tape four lengths together with white floristry tape, leaving 8mm (⅜in) at the bottom. Repeat with the other lengths of wire to make four legs. On each leg spread out the exposed wires to form claws – three

11 Brush the birds with brown dust. Brush the breasts and up over the beak with red dust. Paint the beak grey (mix black and white paste colours). Using the no. 1.5 piping tube, pipe in the eye with royal icing. When the icing is dry, paint black. Place the birds into position on the log.

12 To make the holly follow steps 7–11 on page 108. Place in position by the branch.

13 Stick double-sided tape around the edge of the board and trim with ribbon.

b

8 Coat the bells and clappers with edible glue, then sprinkle them with the coloured glitters (pic d). Shake to remove excess glitter and leave to dry.

9 Place the bells into position on the cake and secure with a little royal icing. Use one small, one medium and one large half bell on the top of the cake. Use two small and one medium half bell around the sides, placing the medium one in the middle. Place the appropriate sized clapper inside each bell on the top of the cake.

10 Place small, thin ribbon bows on the top of each bell, securing with a little royal icing. Stick double-sided tape around the edge of the board and trim with ribbon.

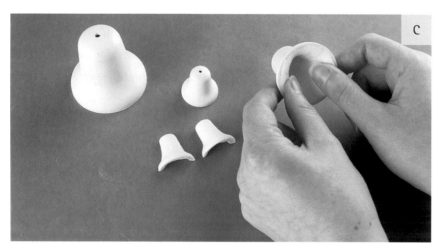

c

piping bag fitted with a no. 1.5 piping tube with the green icing and pipe the branches and needles (pic b). Allow to dry.

6 Use the white modelling paste to make the bells. Roll a ball and dust it with cornflour. Press the ball into the mould and keep the paste moving all the time. Keep removing the paste, re-dusting with cornflour and re-pressing the paste into the mould until a bell shape is formed (pic c). When you're happy with the shape of the bell, remove it from the mould and cut it in half with a sharp knife. You will need one large half bell, five medium half bells and nine small half bells.

7 Prepare the clappers (which are half ball shapes), see step 5, pages 76–77. You will need one large half ball, one medium half ball and one small half ball. Allow all of the moulded elements to dry.

d

New Year
Celebration

It's party time, it's approaching midnight – bring in the new year with balloons, masks, streamers and party blowers.

1 Place the cake on the board. Coat with apricot glaze and cover with marzipan (see page 19).

2 Roll out the white sugarpaste and cover the cake and board (see page 19). Keep any trimmings as you will need to use them later.

3 Roll out the black sugarpaste and cut out numbers 1 to 12 using the number cutters (pic a). Cut out the clock hands using the template on page 155.

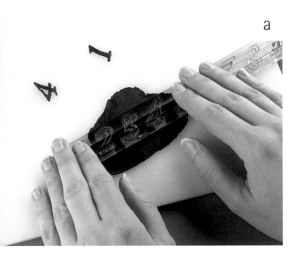

a

Materials

20cm (8in) round light
  fruit cake (see page 11)
Apricot glaze
750g (1lb 10oz) marzipan (almond
  paste) (see page 17)
750g (1lb 10oz) white sugarpaste
  (rolled fondant)
60g (2½oz) red sugarpaste
20g (¾oz) blue sugarpaste
20g (¾oz) green sugarpaste
40g (1½oz) black sugarpaste
20g (¾oz) pink sugarpaste
20g (¾oz) yellow sugarpaste
50g (2oz) modelling paste (see
  page 18)
Paste colours: Christmas red,
  baby blue
Cornflour (cornstarch)
Royal icing (see page 15)

Equipment

28cm (11in) round cake drum
  board
Rolling pin
Sharp knife
Cake smoother
Number cutters
Paintbrush
Face mould
Small pieces of foam
Scissors
Selection of curling ribbons
Greaseproof (waxed) paper piping
  (pastry) bag
No. 1.5 piping tube (nozzle)
Double-sided tape
Red ribbon for cake drum board

b

4 Colour the buttercream with a tiny amount of chestnut brown paste colour to achieve a pale tan colour. Mix well. Using a palette knife, spread the buttercream onto the cake, creating lines that run up and down the bag (pic b).

5 Colour 150g (5½oz) of the modelling paste to the same colour as the buttercream. Roll out the modelling paste and cut out an oval the size of the cake top (where the neck of the bag will be attached). Place onto the cake top. This prevents the buttercream from sticking to the sweets.

6 Roll and cut out a 50 x 5cm (20 x 2in) strip of the tan coloured modelling paste for the neck of the bag and place around the top oval piece, pushing it into the buttercream (pic c). Support the neck with lollipop sticks or similar until it is dry. Place the cake onto the drum board.

7 Colour 35g (1¼oz) of modelling paste with tangerine paste colour and cut out the pumpkin shape using the template on page 155. Mark the segments with a knife (pic d).

8 Colour a very tiny piece of modelling paste green and cut out a stalk shape. Colour the remaining paste black and cut out two eyes, a nose and a mouth (pic d). Place in position on the pumpkin, using

edible glue to secure. Place the pumpkin onto the top of the cake.

9 Fill the neck of the bag with sweets, and spill them out onto the drum board (pic e). Attach cord around the neck of the bag fixing with a little edible glue.

10 Stick double-sided tape around the edge of the drum board and trim with ribbon.

c

d

e

Thanksgiving
Cornucopia

With its assortment of fruit and vegetables, this cake will make a stunning centrepiece for any Thanksgiving table or harvest festival.

1 If you have baked an oval cake you first need to shape it. Trace the template on page 156 onto greaseproof paper and place on top of the cake. Carefully cut the cake into the teardrop shape.

2 Round off the sides of the cake. At the front of the teardrop cut downwards to shape the platform on which the fruit and vegetables will be placed (pic a). Place the cake onto the drum board, allowing space at the front of the cake for the fruit and vegetables.

3 Roll seven sausages of marzipan, each one long enough to wrap over the cake. They will need to vary in length according to the tapering of the horn shape. Flatten them and place over the cake leaving more space between them at the wider end of the cake (pic b). When covered, these will create the ridges in the horn.

Materials

25cm (10in) teardrop, or 25cm (10in) oval, light or rich fruit cake (see pages 11 and 12)
750g (1½lb) marzipan (almond paste) (for covering cake) (see page 17)
750g (1½lb) marzipan (almond paste) (for fruits and vegetables)
Apricot glaze
Gold lustre
Paste colours: spruce green, gooseberry, christmas red, melon, tangerine, grape violet, chestnut brown, christmas green
Small amount of white sugarpaste (rolled fondant)
Royal icing (for fixing elements in place) (see page 15)

Equipment

40cm (16in) oval cake drum board
Greaseproof (waxed) paper
Sharp knife
Rolling pin
Pastry brush
Dresden tool
Dusting brush
Star tool
Fine nutmeg grater
Small calyx cutter
Rose petal cutters
Primrose leaf veiner
Double-sided tape
Lilac ribbon for cake drum board

4 Brush the cake with warm apricot glaze. Roll out the marzipan into a long oval, about 5mm (¼in) thick. Place it onto the cake and smooth it down and into the ridges.

Trim off the excess and, with a dresden tool, press the ridges gently to define the shape. Dust the ridges with gold lustre using a soft brush.

5 For the fruits and vegetables start by combining any remaining marzipan from the cake covering with the quantity for the fruits and vegetables. Colour a small amount of marzipan with each of the paste colours listed on page 124. Leave a small amount uncoloured.

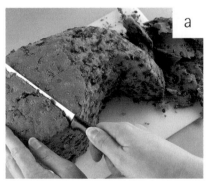

6 For the fruits (pic c, see page 126):
Apples – roll small balls of spruce and gooseberry green. Indent the top with the dresden tool and add a small stalk and leaf.
Plums and apricots – use ovals of grape violet and tangerine. Use a dresden tool to draw a line down one side, add a stalk.
Pears – roll a small ball of spruce green. Roll the paste between your fingers to form the neck. Roll on your little finger to form the waist. Use the star tool to indent the base and add a stalk to the top.
Lemons – roll a ball of melon yellow. Squeeze each end into a slight point. Use a star tool to indent the stalk

8 Pipe the red and white stripes. Each stripe should be comprised of four rows of piped stars. Keep the stars as neat as possible. Allow to dry.

5 Spread white buttercream around the sides of the cake. Use an icing comb to texture each side (pic a).

6 Mark the top of the cake to form guidelines for your icing. Divide it into eight equal strips and mark in the rectangle in the top left-hand

corner, approximately 10 x 12cm (4 x 4½in).

7 Fit the star tubes into the piping bags and fill with blue, red and white buttercream. Pipe the blue rectangle first. Pipe in even rows, keeping the stars a similar size (pic b).

9 Colour a small amount of buttercream with melon paste colour. Pipe small yellow stars onto the blue rectangle (pic c).

Father's Day
TV

Forget the cards and presents, Dad likes to sit back, with the remote control in his hand, and watch sport on TV.

1 If you want to colour your own sugarpaste rather than buying it ready-coloured, do this first. Wrap each piece separately in clingfilm to prevent it drying out.

2 Dampen the drum board with a little water. Roll out the teddy bear brown sugarpaste and cover the board (see page 20). Texture the paste using the bark embosser (pic a).

Materials

25cm (10in) square madeira cake (see page 13)

750g (1lb 10oz) teddy bear brown sugarpaste (rolled fondant)

1 quantity buttercream (see page 14)

750g (1lb 10oz) red sugarpaste

100g (3¼oz) white sugarpaste

135g (4½oz) atlantic blue sugarpaste

65g (2¾oz) baby blue sugarpaste

10g (½oz) black sugarpaste

150g (5oz) grey sugarpaste

10g (½oz) dark green sugarpaste

100g (3¼oz) brown sugarpaste

Paste colours: black, green, red, blue, brown, chestnut brown

Edible glue

Royal icing (see page 15)

Clear alcohol

Equipment

30cm (12in) square cake drum board

Rolling pin

Sharp knife

Cake smoother

Bark embosser

Veining tool

Paintbrushes

Shell tool

No. 2 piping tube (nozzle)

Small piece of foam

Double-sided tape

Red ribbon for cake drum board

a

glue and indent with the end of a paintbrush. Fix the nose into place. Use the tip of a knife to mark the mouth.

16 To make the hat, use a small amount of bottle green sugarpaste and roll it into a ball. Flatten it slightly at the top and bottom. Make a long sausage for the brim and place it around the top of the hat. Place the hat on the head.

17 For the fishing rod cut a 14cm (5½in) length of the green wire, bend one end, and a 25cm (10in) length of silver wire. Bind the two wires together with four short lengths of silver wire (pic d).

18 Place the rod in the fisherman's hands while the paste is still soft. Secure with a little royal icing if necessary. Place the boat onto the cake and secure with royal icing.

19 To make the fish use white sugarpaste coloured with autumn leaf paste colour. Make a selection of fish in varying sizes or use the templates on page 157. Place around the sides of the cake. Put the end of the fishing line into the mouth of one of the larger fish.

20 Roll lots of pebbles from leftover sugarpaste and scatter around the drum board.

21 Roll and cut out a selection of green circles for lily pads, cut out a 'V' section with the back of a knife (pic d). Place on the top of the cake securing into position with royal icing.

22 Using royal icing coloured with mint green paste colour, pipe a selection of weeds up the sides of the cake using the No. 1.5 piping tube (pic e).

23 With white royal icing pipe a few ripples and bubbles around the boat and fish.

24 Stick double-sided tape around the edge of the drum board and trim with ribbon.

Good Luck
Shamrocks

This cake could be suitable for so many celebrations – a new job, to wish someone bon voyage and, of course, St Patrick's Day.

1 Coat the cake in apricot glaze and cover with marzipan (see page 19). Place the prepared cake onto the drum board and cover the cake and board with primrose sugarpaste (see page 19). With the veining tool, texture the paste on the drum, rolling the tool back and forth.

2 Roll out the green sugarpaste and start cutting out the small hearts (pic a). Place them in groups of three, to form the shamrock shape, evenly around the sides of the cake. You will need approximately 72 in total but do not cut them all at once as they will dry out.

Materials

20cm (8in) trefoil shaped light fruit
   cake (see page 11)
Apricot glaze
675g (1½lb) marzipan (almond
   paste) (see page 17)
675g (1½lb) primrose sugarpaste
   (rolled fondant)
75g (3oz) lincoln green sugarpaste

Equipment

25cm (10in) trefoil cake drum board

Rolling pin
Cake smoother
Sharp knife
Veining tool
Heart plunger cutter
Small pieces of foam
Small bowl
Greaseproof (waxed) paper piping
   (pastry) bag
No. 1.5 piping tube (nozzle)
Double-sided tape
Yellow ribbon for cake drum board

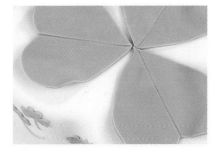

a

3 With the remaining green sugarpaste, roll and cut out three large hearts using the template on page 158 (pic b). Mark a central vein in each one using the back of a knife.

4 Leave the hearts to dry, lifting the edges slightly with a little foam to curl the leaves (pic c).

5 Put a small piece of green sugarpaste into a bowl and add a little water. Mash the paste until you achieve a smooth, piping consistency. This is going to be used to pipe the stems of the shamrocks and means that the stems will match the leaves exactly.

6 Using a no. 1.5 piping tube, pipe curly stems at the base of each shamrock (pic d).

7 Place the large leaves into position on the top of the cake and secure with a little of the icing.

8 Stick double-sided tape around the edge of the drum board and trim with ribbon.

Congratulations
Gift

This cake would be suitable for almost any occasion. An embossed design is dusted with snowflake lustre to stunning effect.

1 Place the cake on the drum board, coat with warm apricot glaze and cover with marzipan (see page 19).

2 Roll out the sugarpaste and cover the cake and board (see page 19).

3 Crimp the edges of the board.

4 Trace and cut out the template for the cake top on page 158. Place the template in position on the top of the cake (pic a).

Materials

20cm (8in) square rich fruit cake (see page 12)

Apricot glaze

750g (1½lb) marzipan (almond paste) (see page 17)

900g (2lb) white sugarpaste (rolled fondant) (allowing 150g/5½oz for bow)

Snowflake lustre

Small amount of royal icing (see page 15)

Edible glue

Equipment

25cm (10in) square cake drum board

Rolling pin

Cake smoother

Sharp knife

Double curve crimpers

Greaseproof (waxed) paper

Strawberry leaf and calyx cutters

White seed pearls (note: these are not edible; must be removed before cutting and serving)

Fabric textured roller

Small pieces of foam

Double-sided tape

Silver ribbon for cake drum board

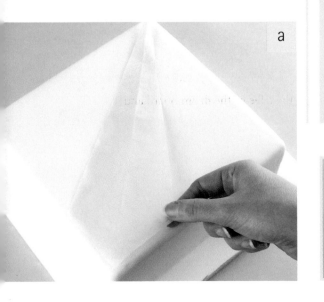

a

5 Using the cutters emboss the top surface of the cake, working around the template. Emboss around the sides of the cake but do not emboss the area at the front corner (imagine you have drawn straight lines down from the two outer points of the template). Finally, emboss the board (pic b). Try not to overlap details, but don't leave any spaces.

6 While the sugarpaste is still soft, gently dust the top and sides of the cake and the board with snowflake

b

lustre. Keep the template in place to prevent the dust from settling on the centre panel.

7 Remove the template and secure the seed pearls in position with a little royal icing. (Remove the pearls before cutting and serving the cake.)

8 To make the bow (pic c) roll out a small amount of sugarpaste and texture with the rolling pin.

9 Trace and cut out the templates on page 158. Cut out four tails, two loops and one knot. For the two bow loops, pleat the ends and fold over. Stick with edible glue. Support the loops with a little foam to help keep the shape when drying.

10 For the knot, pleat the ends and bend over the two loops, trimming off any excess paste.

11 Pleat the tops of the tails.

12 Assemble the pieces together using edible glue and support until dry (pic d).

13 When dry, dust with snowflake lustre and place in position on the top of the cake, securing with a little royal icing.

14 Stick double-sided tape around the edge of the board and trim with silver ribbon.

Tip

When embossing this cake work as quickly as possible as it is best to emboss while the sugarpaste is still soft. Use the same constant pressure and do not press too hard.

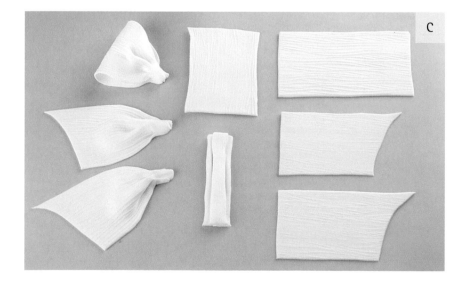

c

d

Templates

All templates are actual size unless otherwise stated.

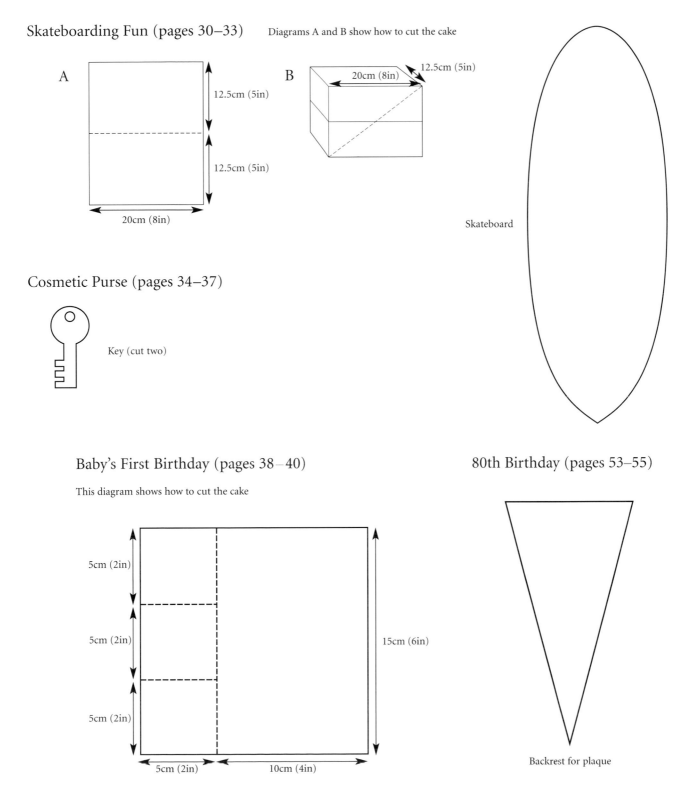

Skateboarding Fun (pages 30–33)

Diagrams A and B show how to cut the cake

A

12.5cm (5in)

12.5cm (5in)

20cm (8in)

B

20cm (8in)

12.5cm (5in)

Skateboard

Cosmetic Purse (pages 34–37)

Key (cut two)

Baby's First Birthday (pages 38–40)

This diagram shows how to cut the cake

5cm (2in)

5cm (2in)

5cm (2in)

15cm (6in)

5cm (2in)   10cm (4in)

80th Birthday (pages 53–55)

Backrest for plaque

Chocolate Wedding Cake (pages 62–64)

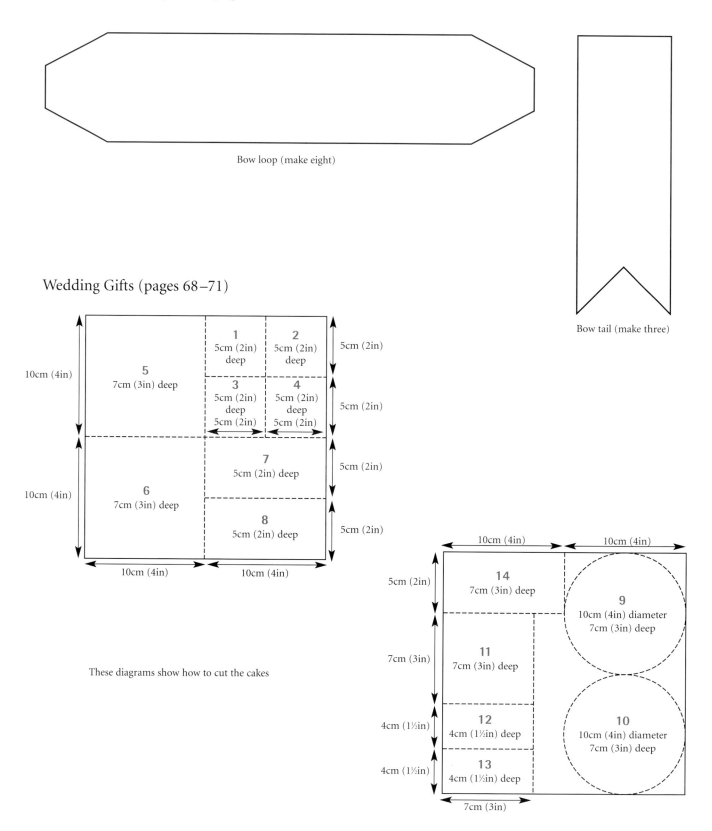

Bow loop (make eight)

Bow tail (make three)

Wedding Gifts (pages 68–71)

These diagrams show how to cut the cakes

Silver Wedding Anniversary (pages 72–75)

Baby Boy's Christening (pages 88–90)

Photocopy at 200%

Ruby Wedding Anniversary (pages 79–81)

Photocopy at 200%

Cushion inner

Cushion cover

Baby Girl's Christening (pages 91–93)

Overall cake shape

Tongue

Photocopy at 200%

This diagram shows how to shape
the cake in step 3

2cm (¾in)

2.5cm
(1in)

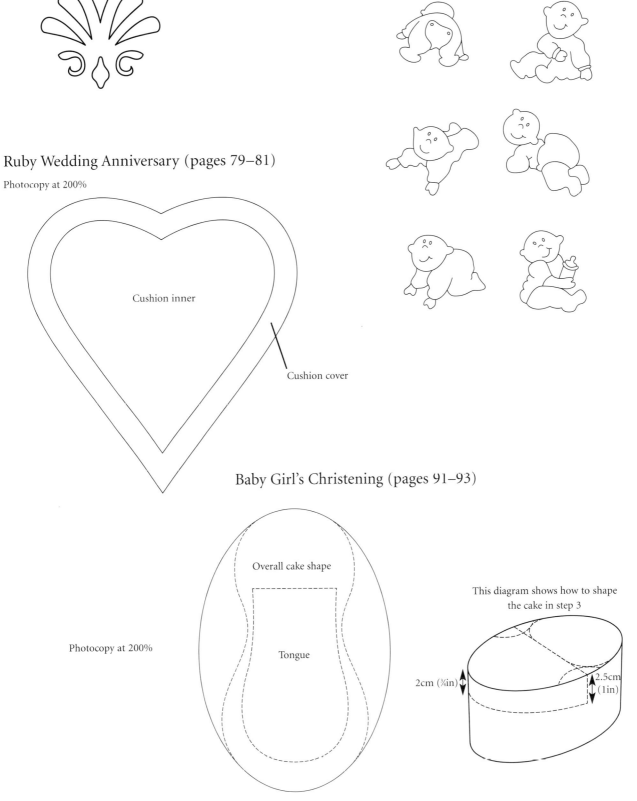

Thanksgiving Cornucopia (pages 124–126)

Photocopy at 200%

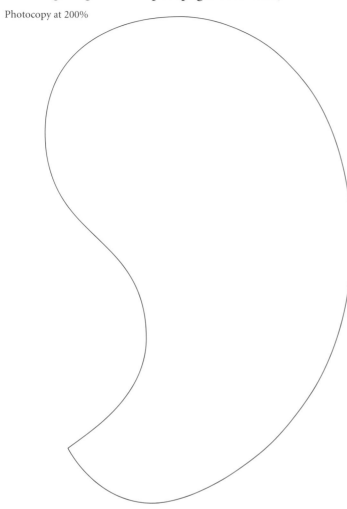

Father's Day TV (pages 134–137)

This diagram shows how to cut the cake

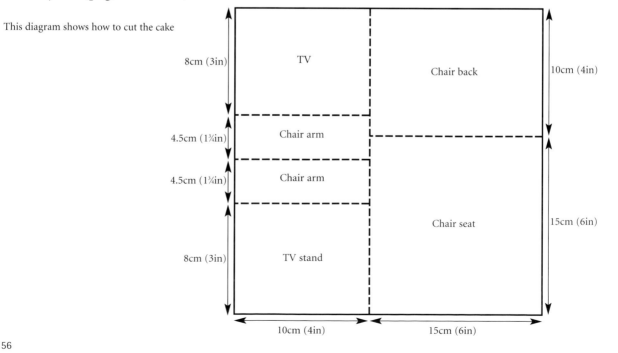

Retirement Fishing Boat (pages 141–144)

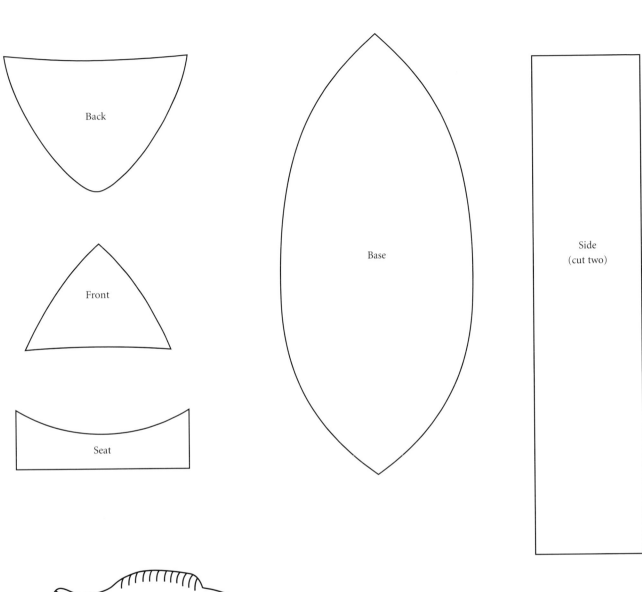

Good Luck Shamrocks (pages 145–147)

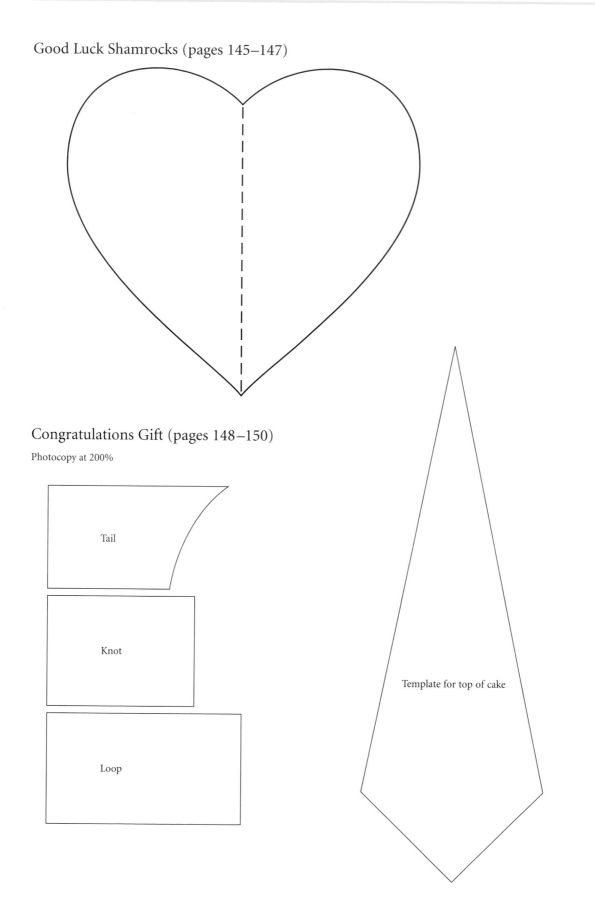

Congratulations Gift (pages 148–150)

Photocopy at 200%

Tail

Knot

Loop

Template for top of cake

Suppliers

UK

Cee for Cakes
Tel: 01525 375237
Fax : 01525 372470
Email: info@ceeforcakes.co.uk
www.ceeforcakes.co.uk

Culpitt Ltd
Jubilee Industrial Estate
Ashington
Northumberland NE63 8UQ
Tel: 01670 814545

FMM Sugarcraft
Unit 5, Kings Park Industrial Estate
Primrose Hill
Kings Langley
Hertfordshire WD4 ST8
Tel: 01923 268699
Fax: 01923 261226
Email: sales@fmmsugarcraft.com
www.fmmsugarcraft.com

Knightsbridge PME
Knightsbridge Bakeware Centre
Chadwell Heath Lane
Romford
Essex RM6 4NP
Tel: 0208 590 5959
Email:
online.orders@cakedecoration.co.uk
www.cakedecoration.co.uk

Renshaw Scott
Sherburn-in-Elmet
Leeds LS25 6JA
Tel: 0870 870 6950
Fax: 0870 870 6951
Email: info@renshawscott.co.uk
www.renshawscott.co.uk

Major Johnson
105 Lakey Lane
Hall Green
Birmingham B28 9DU
Tel: 0121 778 4692

Sugarflair Colours Ltd
Manor Trading Estate
Brunel Road
Benfleet
Essex SS7 4PS
Tel: 01268 752891

Orchard Products
51 Hallyburton Road
Hove
East Sussex BN3 7GP
Tel: 01273 419418
Fax: 01273 412512

Squires Kitchen
Squires House
3 Waverley Lane
Farnham
Surrey GU9 8BB
Tel: 01252 711749
Fax: 01252 714714
Email: productinfo@squires-groups.co.uk
www.squires-group.co.uk

USA/CANADA

Wilton Enterprises
2240 West 75th Street
Woodridge
Illinois 60517
Tel: (+1) 630 963 1818
Fax: (+1) 630 963 7196
www.wilton.com

Wilton Industries Canada
98 Carrier Drive
Etobicoke
Ontario M9W5R1
Tel: (+1) 416 679 0790
Fax: (+1) 416 679 0798

NEW ZEALAND

Decor Cakes Ltd
Victoria Arcade
435 Great South Road
Otahuhu, Auckland
Tel: (09) 276 6676

Innovations Specialty Cookware & Gifts
52 Mokoia Road
Birkenhead, Auckland
Tel: (09) 480 8885

Spotlight
(branches throughout New Zealand)
Wairau Park, 19 Link Drive
Glenfield, Auckland
Tel: (09) 444 0220
www.spotlightonline.co.nz

Sugarcrafts NZ Ltd
99 Queens Road
Panmure
Auckland
Tel: (09) 527 6060

AUSTRALIA

Cake Art Supplies
Kiora Mall
Shop 26 Kiora Rd
MIRANDA
NSW 2228
Tel: (02) 9540 3483

Cake and Icing Centre
651 Samford Rd
MITCHELTON
QLD 4053
Tel: (07) 3355 3443

Petersen's Cake Decorations
370 Cnr South St and Stockdale Rd
OCONNOR
WA 6163
Tel: (08) 9337 9636

SOUTH AFRICA

The Baking Tin
52 Belvedere Road
Claremont
7700
Cape Town
Tel: (021) 671 6434
Stores also in Durban, Bloemfontein,
Skiereiland and Randburg

Jem Cutters
128 Crompton Street
Pinetown 3610
Durban
South Africa
Tel: 031 701 1431
Fax: 031 701 1559

South Bakels
55 Section Street
Paarden Eiland
7420
Cape Town
Tel: (021) 511 1381
Stores also in Johannesburg and
Bloemfontein

Index